The **Essential** Buyer's Guide

# FORD
# MUSTANG

Fifth generation/S197 2005 to 2014

Your marque expert:
Matt Cook

## VELOCE PUBLISHING
THE PUBLISHER OF FINE AUTOMOTIVE BOOKS

# www.veloce.co.uk

For post publication news, updates and amendments relating to this book please visit www.veloce.co.uk/books/V4798

First published in July 2015 by Veloce Publishing Limited, Veloce House, Parkway Farm Business Park, Middle Farm Way, Poundbury, Dorchester, Dorset, DT1 3AR, England.
Fax 01305 250479/e-mail info@veloce.co.uk/web www.veloce.co.uk or www.velocebooks.com.
ISBN: 978-1-845847-98-2 UPC: 6-36847-04798-6
Readers with ideas for automotive books, or books on other transport or related hobby subjects, are invited to write to the editorial director of Veloce Publishing at the above address.
British Library Cataloguing in Publication Data – A catalogue record for this book is available from the British Library.
Typesetting, design and page make-up all by Veloce Publishing Ltd on Apple Mac. Printed in India by Imprint Digital Ltd

# Introduction
– the purpose of this book

Iconic, stylish and sporty, the Ford Mustang has been an object of desire since its launch in 1964, and continues to be Ford's flagship performance car that is still seen on the showroom floors throughout the world today. The 2005 Mustang, with its strong, muscular and retro styling, caused quite a stir with the motoring press when it was first unveiled at the Detroit (NAIAS) auto show in January 2004.

Since its launch the S197 Mustang has gained devoted fans the world over, and reinforced the image of the Ford Mustang. (Courtesy Ford Motor Company)

Many enthusiasts feel the S197 was the best pony car to come out of the US motor city for decades. The people seemed to agree, buying over 159,000 Mustangs during 2005. As in the 1960s, Ford left both GM and Chrysler with some catching up to do. With two major styling changes and an entirely new drivetrain, at the end of the 2014 production run, Ford had sold over 1.1 million S197 Mustangs in North America.

Very few cars have enjoyed the 50+ year lifespan of the Mustang, even fewer share the same colorful history and iconic status as a symbol of performance and a slice of Americana. With two body styles, different paint colors, deluxe and premium interior trim options, styling and handling upgrades, different engine, transmission, and many other options. You could have Ford build your Mustang at the state-of-the-art Flat Rock assembly plant in Michigan, and deliver it to your local dealer after you ticked off the options list. Values can vary greatly between models, and variations depend on what was checked off on that options sheet by the original owner. Usually, if the condition is equal, a well-optioned convertible will demand a higher value than a coupe. However, the muscular coupe was the most popular and, arguably, most practical body-style of all, easily outselling the convertible.

The unveiling of the S197 Mustang at the 2004 NAIAS in Detroit: it was an instant hit with the public.

While this book is applicable to any 2005-2014 Mustang, it does not specifically cover those not made by Ford Motor Co, such as the highly desirable models from Roush, Saleen, Steeda or Shelby American. If you're in the market for one of these high-performance ponies, this book will still be a useful reference but won't cover the unique features of those models.

While 2005-2009 models have the strongest visual ties, this 2013 Boss 302 and 1968 fastback share more than just a passing resemblance.

While the S197 Mustang is commonplace within the USA and Canada, there are fans of Ford's great pony car the world over who enjoy the fun and excitement these vehicles bring to motoring, and the equally vibrant club, show and motorsport scenes they're associated with.

This book is not an exhaustive list of all available options and features; it's a guide for when you're viewing a potential purchase, aimed at those who want a safe, clean, solid and reliable car to enjoy and drive.

# Contents

**THE ESSENTIAL BUYER'S GUIDE™ CURRENCY**
At the time of publication a BG unit of currency "●" equals approximately US$1.00
/£0.64/Euro 0.90. Please adjust to suit current exchange rates using the US Dollar
as the base rate.

# 1 Is it the right car for you?
– marriage guidance

The largest S197 Mustang is just under 16ft long and just over 6½ft wide, so an average single car garage of 18ft x 8ft (5.5m x 2.5m) should be sufficient for most.

Both body styles have enough room for four seated adults, however, leg room behind a tall driver is limited. Drivers of smaller stature may find the high-level dashboard

Spacious and comfortable, the interior of this 2005 Mustang GT convertible is a cool place to be, especially with the top down.

makes the car feel big, and might wish to have a higher seating position. The seats have plenty of adjustment to find a comfortable position. The trunk can swallow two large suitcases and a soft hold-all, less if the optional subwoofer is fitted.

The power assisted steering has a weighty feel, but offers plenty of assistance when parking. The four-wheel disc brakes feel responsive, particularly on models with the Brembo front calipers. The clutch on manual transmission cars is on the heavy side with a long pedal action, while all automatics are easy to live with. The emergency brake is mounted to the left of the transmission tunnel, and can feel a little awkward to some.

All models are high-performance machines and can easily keep up with traffic, all variants are competent and practical cruisers for long-distance trips. They are however, vulnerable to car-park damage and always draw (usually admiring) attention. As with all powerful rear-wheel drive cars, drivers should take care when making turns, as there can be a tendency to oversteer.

All variants of the S197 Mustang have larger capacity engines when compared to their European and Japanese counterparts, which equates to higher factory fuel consumption figures. Good parts availability helps to keep servicing costs low, and means that S197 Mustangs can be cheap to run and maintain.

If using specialist insurers, insurance costs can be very reasonable for standard cars. Modified cars are obviously more expensive, and may need to be considered on an individual basis. Outside of the USA and Canada, using a specialist insurer is normally your best option.

S197 Mustangs hold their value well within their market segment, with vehicle values being notably higher outside of the USA and Canada.

Direct alternatives would be the Chevrolet Camaro and Dodge Challenger.

# 2 Cost considerations
– affordable, or a money pit?

Service intervals: Every 5000 miles (8000km) or 6 months under normal conditions.
Small service: ●x200
Large service: ●x350
Rebuilt/replacement engine:
●x3500 to ●x20,000
Rebuilt/replacement transmission:
●x2300 to ●x5200
Brake disc cost: ●x40 to ●x80 front each/●x35 to ●x50 rear each
Brake pad cost: ●x30 to ●x60 front/●x30 to ●x50 rear
New front fender (wing) cost: ●x350
Front bumper cover: ●x420
Rear bumper cover: ●x230 to ●x630
New headlight cost: ●x150 to ●x275
Full respray (incl preparation):
●x3000 to ●x10,000

Most parts, oils and lubricants are easy to find throughout the USA and Canada. Outside of these regions consulting specialist suppliers may be your best option.

These are the standard two-piston aluminum calipers from a 2005 GT. Second-hand parts can be a cost effective alternative to new items.

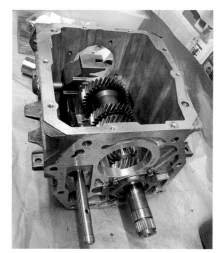

With a ready supply of new, reproduction and used parts, owning and maintaining an S197 Mustang isn't expensive. These used front struts and springs were a bargain.

This T5 5-speed manual transmission has been torn down for inspection and rebuild. All manual transmissions only require regular routine fluid changes as directed by Ford.

# 3 Living with a Mustang
– will you get along together?

A 2005-2014 Mustang is both a pleasure to own and drive. With the aftermarket parts industries in the US and Canada offering great support for these vehicles, you can buy almost anything; from custom interior trim, performance brakes, suspension packages, through to a supercharger kit which can turn an average pony into a full blown thoroughbred. The car's fantastic following means that parts availability is as good as ever, making the S197 Mustang an excellent choice for a would-be American performance car owner.

While perfectly suited to daily driver duty, some people still prefer to enjoy their Mustang primarily on weekends, high-days and holidays. Some Mustang owners, particularly in colder and wetter climates, choose to keep their cars garaged or stored under a cover in the winter months.

Due to the ever increasing fuel and oil prices, Ford has kept the Mustang updated in line with the very latest governmental fuel economy and emissions standards, resulting in a vehicle which is every bit as powerful as the original 1960s icons that inspired it, but with far greater efficiency and reliability.

With what we've all come to expect from modern, super-efficient, computer-controlled, fuel-injected machines, a figure below 35mpg can often be expected. Compared to an average family sedan, all S197 Mustangs have relatively large-capacity engines.

The six-cylinder engines are less thirsty than their V8 stablemates, but even the trusty V6 is behind mpg figures offered by the latest generation of small-engine economy focused vehicles. This said, the S197 easily matches or often exceeds the efficiency of other vehicles with similar performance, even when compared to its European or Japanese counterparts. The higher fuel consumption, as with any performance vehicle, is far outweighed by the grin factor which is offered in return.

Driven day-to-day these machines are robust and extremely reliable. Like all vehicles, they do require regular routine maintenance and servicing, but most operations are easily undertaken by a professional automotive technician or an even by an enthusiastic owner. These cars are easy to work on, and are often far simpler than their European or Japanese counterparts.

With four comfortable seats, a reasonably sized trunk (which also houses the spare wheel) and plenty of horsepower, Mustangs can be both practical and comfortable tourers. With plush cloth or easy to clean leather seats, dark carpets, door panels and headliner in a complementary factory color scheme, all come together to produce a modern but retro-inspired theme to the interior.

All of the important gauges and controls are easily visible and accessible from the driving seat. Forward visibility over the high dashboard and down the long hood/bonnet is good, although a higher seating position may be required for drivers of smaller stature. Lateral views are more restricted on the coupe due to the large B-pillar, and are also more limited with the convertible top up. Rear visibility is good, but the spoiler, when fitted, can obscure the view over the high deck-lid. The coupe is the more practical body style and definitely has the more muscular look, but it just won't have the same appeal for those who love convertibles.

With both manual and automatic transmission options, there's a Mustang to suit most drivers. The 5-speed and 6-speed manual transmissions can be great fun, although the factory shifter doesn't like to be rushed, and hearing some transmission noise is normal. The standard clutch has a longer action and gives a really positive engagement.

The excellent Ford five-speed and later six-speed electronically-controlled automatic transmissions will have you gliding along quickly and effortlessly, delivering many miles of trouble-free motoring, if well maintained with regular servicing and routine fluid changes.

Even though the suspension design of the S197 Mustang has been described by many as being outdated and even antiquated, this doesn't prevent the Mustang from being a nice, responsive and often fun car to drive. Similarly, not many suspension designs and associated drivetrains can handle the onslaught of 500 or more supercharged horsepower that a Shelby GT500 can throw at them, all with a factory-backed warranty.

Arguably, it's those same underpinnings that have allowed the S197 Mustang to be a success on the streets, at the drag strips and on the road courses across America.

**This splendid white pony offers its owner the perfect mix of performance, fun and practicality, making it a great companion, even, as here, in the English countryside! (Courtesy Ray Welch)**

# 4 Relative values
– which model for you?

As a general rule the biggest factors affecting the value of an S197 Mustang are the model variant, followed by condition, age and mileage; any performance related options or upgrades, then finally trim or convenience options.

The 2005 Mustang GT, the first of a new breed. The 300hp V8 and retro-styling made it an instant success with the American public and Mustang fans the world over. (Courtesy Ray Welch)

All else being equal, convertible cars usually command higher prices than their coupe brethren, but there's no doubt that the more muscular-looking coupe is more popular.

A V8 GT will almost always command more than the equivalent base V6 model. Similarly, a 2006 model versus a 2005 will also usually be of a higher value. Lastly, a GT with premium options will manage only a slightly higher value versus a lesser-optioned car.

Performance-related options and upgrades can sometimes buck the market

This 2006 V6 coupe is a great and practical daily driver, and looks the part, too. The classic retro styled 16in Halibrand replica wheels and spinners really suit the car.
(Courtesy Ray Welch)

This clean and tidy 2006 Mustang V6 convertible is perfect for some top-down fun.
(Courtesy Ray Welch)

The quintessential Ford Mustang is a red GT convertible. This example is a nice stock-appearing car that will deliver many smiles per mile.

This Shelby GT500KR is one of only a handful built to commemorate the 40th anniversary of the 1968 original. With 540hp, it truly is a 'King of the Road.'
(Courtesy Alex Fearn)

Looking resplendent in Kona blue, this 2010 V6 Premium Coupe is the last year with 4.0L SOHC V6 engine. (Courtesy Ray Welch)

The 2011 GT saw the introduction of the 412hp 5.0L Ti-VCT V8 nicknamed 'Coyote' after the engineering name. The tell-tale sign is the 5.0 badge on the front fender. (Courtesy Ray Welch)

With fewer than 560 examples built, the Kona blue and white 2012 Mustang Boss 302 is bound to become a future collector's item. (Courtesy Ray Welch)

This stunning school bus yellow 2013 Mustang Boss 302 sits alongside a replica of its namesake the North American P-51 Mustang. (Courtesy Ray Welch)

This 2013 Shelby GT500 is eye-popping, both in hue and performance. (Courtesy Ray Welch)

Just as comfortable on the show field as the open road, this 2014 V6 Mustang Club of America edition looks right at home. A future classic? (Courtesy Ray Welch)

trend. For example, for some buyers having the desirable 'Brembo brake package' option on a 2011+ GT would be a must-have feature, which outweighs other factors like vehicle age or higher mileage.

On page 11 is a value matrix providing a rough overview of S197 values. A baseline for each table is the newest vehicle which will likely demand the highest value (signified as [0] in the table) with progressive value deductions for each year and model. Considerations for average mileage and depreciation have been factored in.

Start with 100% and subtract the figures shown below. For example: If you're looking at a 2013 V8 GT coupe, calculate the relative value thus:

Model = **-16%**
**TOTAL = 100% - 16% = 84%**

So, if a 2014 GT convertible is worth circa ⬤x31,000, then a 2013 GT coupe might roughly be worth ⬤x26,040 by comparison.

Of course, at the time of writing, these cars are still recent enough to feature in the sort of modern car value guides sold on news stands.

## Mustang base (V6) models

| Model | 2005 | 2006 | 2007 | 2008 | 2009 | 2010 | 2011 | 2012 | 2013 | 2014 |
|---|---|---|---|---|---|---|---|---|---|---|
| V6 coupe | -61% | -57% | -55% | -52% | -48% | -33% | -29% | -24% | -12% | -5% |
| V6 convertible | -61% | -56% | -52% | -45% | -43% | -31% | -24% | -19% | -10% | [0] |

## Mustang GT (V8) models

| Model | 2005 | 2006 | 2007 | 2008 | 2009 | 2010 | 2011 | 2012 | 2013 | 2014 |
|---|---|---|---|---|---|---|---|---|---|---|
| GT coupe | -66% | -65% | -58% | -52% | -45% | -39% | -29% | -22% | -16% | -10% |
| GT convertible | -58% | -55% | -52% | -42% | -39% | -29% | -19% | -13% | -6% | [0] |
| Bullitt | | | | -39% | -35% | | | | | |

## Boss 302

| Model | 2005 | 2006 | 2007 | 2008 | 2009 | 2010 | 2011 | 2012 | 2013 | 2014 |
|---|---|---|---|---|---|---|---|---|---|---|
| Boss 302 | | | | | | | | -20% | -15% | |
| Boss 302 Laguna Seca | | | | | | | | -5% | [0] | |

## Shelby GT500

| Model | 2005 | 2006 | 2007 | 2008 | 2009 | 2010 | 2011 | 2012 | 2013 | 2014 |
|---|---|---|---|---|---|---|---|---|---|---|
| Shelby GT500 coupe | | | -53% | -50% | -50% | -45% | -40% | -40% | -15% | -5% |
| Shelby GT500 convertible | | | -52% | -50% | -42% | -40% | -35% | -35% | -10% | [0] |

The limited 40th anniversary edition Shelby GT500KR should be considered independently, due to its collector car status.

# 5 Before you view
– be well informed

To avoid a wasted journey, and the disappointment of finding that the car does not match your expectations, it will help if you're very clear about what questions you want to ask before you pick up the telephone. Some of these points might appear basic, but when you're excited about the prospect of buying your dream Mustang, it's amazing how some of the most obvious things slip the mind. Also check the current values of the model you are interested in within car trader magazines and on the internet, which give both a price guide and auction results.

## Where is the car?
Is it going to be worth travelling to the next county/state, or even across a border? A local car, although it may not sound very interesting, can add to your knowledge for very little effort, so make a visit – it might even be in better condition than expected.

## Dealer or private sale?
Establish early on if the car is being sold by its owner or by a trader. The owner should have all the history, so don't be afraid to ask detailed questions. A dealer may have more limited knowledge of the car, but should have some documentation. A dealer may offer a warranty/guarantee (ask for a printed copy) and finance.

## Cost of collection & delivery?
A dealer may well be used to quoting for delivery by car transporter. A private owner may agree to meet you halfway, but only agree to this after you have seen the car at the vendor's address to validate the documents. Conversely, you could meet halfway and agree the sale but insist on meeting at the vendor's address for the handover.

## View – when & where?
It is always preferable to view at the vendor's home or business premises. In the case of a private sale, the car's documentation should tally with the vendor's name and address. Arrange to view only in daylight and avoid a wet day. Most cars look better in poor light or when wet.

## Reason for sale?
Do make it one of the first questions. Why is the car being sold and how long has it been with the current owner? How many previous owners?

Ford never built a regular production S197 Mustang with RHD from the factory. If a RHD conversion has been done well (conversions were required by law in Australia until recently), it is possible that the specific vehicle could be worth more, compared to a standard LHD variant in certain countries, where RHD is the norm.

## Condition?
Ask for an honest appraisal of the car's condition. Ask specifically about some of the check items described in Chapters 8 and 9.

## All original specification?
An original equipment car is usually more desirable, but this may not be the case, as

many S197 Mustangs may have been modified or customised by their owners, so consider each vehicle on its own individual merit.

## Matching data/legal ownership

Do VIN/chassis, engine numbers and licence plate match the registration document? Are the owner's name and address recorded in the registration documents?

For those countries that require an annual test of roadworthiness, does the car have a document showing it complies (an MoT certificate in the UK, which can be verified on 0845 600 5977)?

If a smog/emissions certificate is mandatory, does the car have one?

If required, does the car carry a current road fund license/licence plate tag?

Does the vendor own the car outright? Money might be owed to a finance company or bank: the car could even be stolen. Several organisations will supply the data on ownership, based on the car's licence plate number, for a fee. Such companies can often also tell you whether the car has been 'written-off' by an insurance company. In the UK these organisations can supply vehicle data:

HPI – 01722 422 422
AA – 0870 600 0836
DVLA – 0870 240 0010
RAC – 0870 533 3660

Other countries will have similar organisations.

## Insurance

Check with your existing insurer before setting out, your current policy might not cover you to drive the car if you do purchase it.

## How you can pay

In Europe, money laundering rules preclude the use of cash transactions for vehicles of a certain value. Some desirable S197 models in good condition can exceed the permitted amount, so remind the seller of this if they request a cash transaction.

A cheque/check will take several days to clear and the seller may prefer to sell to a cash buyer. However, a banker's draft (a cheque issued by a bank) is as good as cash, but safer, so contact your own bank and become familiar with the formalities that are necessary to obtain one.

## Buying at auction?

If the intention is to buy at auction see Chapter 10 for further advice.

## Professional vehicle check (mechanical examination)

Marque/model specialists will undertake professional examination of a vehicle on your behalf. Owners clubs will be able to put you in touch with such specialists. Other organisations that will carry out a general professional check in the UK are:

AA – 0800 085 3007 (motoring organisation with vehicle inspectors)
ABS – 0800 358 5855 (specialist vehicle inspection company)
RAC – 0870 533 3660 (motoring organisation with vehicle inspectors)

Other countries will have similar organisations.

# 6 Inspection equipment

– these items will really help

## This book

Before you rush out of the door, gather together a few items that will help as you work your way around the car. This book is designed to be your guide at every step, so take it along and use the check boxes to help you assess each area of the car you're interested in. Don't be afraid to let the seller see you using it.

## Reading glasses (if you need them for close work)

Don't forget to take your reading glasses if you need them to read documents and make close up inspections. Your most important tools when looking over a car are your own eyes, pay close attention to even the smallest detail.

## Flashlight (with fresh batteries)

A flashlight with fresh batteries will be useful for peering into the engine bay, into the wheel arches and under the rest of the car.

## Overalls

Be prepared to get dirty. Take along a pair of overalls, if you have them.

## Mirror on a stick

Fixing a mirror at an angle on the end of a stick may seem odd, but you'll probably need it to check the condition of the underside of the car. It will also help you to peer into some of the important crevices. You can also use it, together with the flashlight, along the underside of the rocker panels and floor to check for damage.

## Digital camera

If you have the use of a digital camera, take it along so that later you can study some areas of the car more closely. Take a picture of any part of the car that causes you concern, and seek a friend's advice or opinion. Don't forget to take a photo of the VIN and door data decals, as these can help you to find out the original factory specification.

## Pen & paper

Use these details to note down the registration details, mileage, VIN number, tire sizes and other particulars. This allows you to refer to online resources later to verify the original build specification, options installed or even to find out how much replacement tires will cost.

## A friend, preferably a knowledgeable enthusiast

Ideally, have a friend or knowledgeable enthusiast accompany you – a second opinion is always valuable.

# 7 Fifteen minute evaluation
– walk away or stay?

If you've never viewed or driven a Mustang or similar car before, it's difficult not to get caught up by the muscle car image and sheer road presence. Add to the mix the allure and excitement of hearing that V8 rumble or the V6 purr, and you'll be proverbial putty in the seller's hands before you know it. While for some it may be an emotional, heart-felt decision to buy a Mustang, it's important to not let your heart rule your head when viewing a car, or you might end up driving home in a lemon.

While legalities and the accepted level of roadworthiness varies from country to country, it'd be naïve to rely on this basic approval alone. A good example is the UK, where the annual MoT roadworthiness test inspects a multitude of items, including structural integrity of the vehicle. But these inspections are usually limited by time and what is actually permitted as part of the inspection. Badly damaged or poorly repaired cars can be disguised with body filler (bondo) and a rattle can paint job.

Start with the body and structural condition of the car. The most expensive mistake you can make is to buy a lovely looking car with nice interior trim and great sounding engine, but has suffered accident damage or poor repairs which can require expensive remedial work.

Pay particular attention to the character lines of the body, these should be sharp, defined, but more importantly, they should match up when looking the length of the car. Look at the vehicle both directly head-on and tail-on. Check for even lines on both sides, and symmetry between the driver side and the passenger side, all lines should be equal. If the panels seem somewhat uneven or distorted it could indicate previous accident damage or poor workmanship when repairing the vehicle.

Checking the floors, chassis rails and other structures from underneath requires the use of those bin-liners, overalls and a torch/flashlight.

The forward chassis rail sections start at the radiator panel, and extend back to the firewall where they angle downwards under the floors. These must be perfectly straight and true, as these sections are designed to crumple in a frontal impact.

Make sure you walk around the whole car looking for symmetry, even panel gaps, and character lines that should flow the length of the car without any misalignment.

Also check underneath for damage to the K-member, oil pan or exhaust system tubing, possibly caused by grounding or impact with a raised drain cover or kerb.

Check the front bumper cover fits properly and doesn't seem to be loose or have large gaps, as this can indicate broken fixings from a minor incident. This is especially important on models with splitters (Boss or Shelby models) or protruding bumper designs.

At the rear, also check the rear bumper cover fitment and associated diffuser on some models. Again, any misalignment, scratches or indentations to the softer plastic is usually evidence of a minor reversing incident. Check low down as well, as many people forget the overhang, and can cause damage if close to a high kerb.

The rear lower sections of the rear bumper facia and the rear of the front fender and side skirt behind the wheel can suffer from debris being picked up by the spinning wheel, so pay close attention, looking for paint chips and other damage.

Look at the side skirts from low down, as scratches and damage can be easily overlooked here.

Check all glass on the vehicle, as obtaining replacements can be expensive, particularly if you're outside of the continental US or Canada. Door glass can suffer from vertical scratches if dirt or grit is lodged between the glass and window seals.

The chassis number or VIN is visible on the driver-side (LH) lower section of the windshield. Note it down with your pen and paper or take a photo so you can decode it later.

When opening the doors, the power window drops the glass slightly to clear the upper edge of the window channel seals. The power windows have a soft open/close feature and should cleanly drop without noise or resistance to the fully open position.

Some early cars did have an issue with the exterior door handle retracting: there's a Technical Service Bulletin (TSB) issued by Ford to resolve this.

With driver-side door open look for the data tag, it's a self-adhesive sticker on the B-pillar. Take a photo or note it down for reference. Begin to question what you have if the data-sticker is missing or has been painted over by a poorly masked/executed paint job.

Door shuts are also good little tell-tale areas for paint or body repairs as they tend to catch overspray. Check thoroughly near the door hinges for overspray, or poorly adhered paint. Masking tape lines and uneven paint surfaces in these areas can quickly tell you if there's been a lot of love, or little attention given. Be especially wary if the seller has told you this car is an unmolested car, but you find evidence indicating otherwise.

The bottoms and lower outer skins of the doors are likely to suffer from future corrosion issues, so be sure to check from underneath.

Visually inspect all of the road wheels, checking for kerb damage and corrosion, particularly on wheels with machined aluminum lips or spokes. Refurbishing or replacing road wheels can be expensive. Look at the tire treads, checking for sufficient tread and even wear.

While checking the wheels, also try to look at the color and condition of the brake rotors (discs): blueing can indicate overheated or warped rotors caused by over-zealous driving, seized brake caliper pistons, or even seized parking brake cables if on the rear. The discs should be evenly worn and free from large grooves or ridges.

While looking into the wheelarches, check for perished or split rubber gaiters and ball joint covers. Check the control arms and trackrods for straightness at the front, and the stabilizer, end-links and panhard bar are secure at the rear.

Pop the hood by pulling the release lever located in the driver's side footwell. The hood safety latch is in the centre, just above the grille. Lift and safely secure with the hood prop rod.

With the bonnet/hood open, check for signs of overspray

The VIN is displayed at the base of the windshield on the driver's side. Make a quick note of this, or snap a photo so you can decode it later.

The driver's door pillar contains several data labels as shown. These are useful cross reference points, and may be an indication of prior paint repairs if they're missing.

and poor masking around the edges of the hood, fender tops, strut towers, hood hinges and inner fenders.

All S197 Mustangs had aluminum hoods from the factory, in order to save weight. Unfortunately these can suffer from corrosion, particularly on the leading edge of the hood. With the hood open, pay close attention to the underside leading edge, as this is the first area that will show signs of corrosion in the form of paint blistering.

Take some overall photos of the engine bay: this will allow you to refer back later if necessary. Checking for the general appearance, condition, and listening out for problems is more important in your allotted time. Pay particular attention to things like the routing of wiring looms and hoses, as these should all be nicely laid out and retained in their factory positions. If not, it could indicate that some remedial work has been done, or even that the engine has been out at some point. Thoroughly check for leaks or dirty areas where dust and grime accumulate around oily or greasy substances.

**Look closely at the wheels, possibly even take a photo. From one simple shot you can verify the tire size, wheel condition, caliper type, and even the rotor color/ condition.**

While looking in the engine bay, check that all fluid levels are within limits. Keep in mind that the coolant will be hot and the system may be pressurised if the owner has run the engine beforehand. The coolant/radiator caps are known to fail, so look for signs of weeping or evidence of staining. S197 Mustangs don't have automatic transmission fluid dipsticks, so you'll have to be more vigilant on the test drive.

Check the brake fluid level, and look for evidence of fluid or peeled paint underneath the master cylinder: this could indicate a leak from the cap or one of the unions/pipes. Obviously, if there's evidence of a leak, don't drive the car as it could be dangerous.

If looking in the engine bay with the engine running, be aware of the spinning pulleys and drivebelts, as they can do some serious harm to you. Listen for rattling, ticking or knocking sounds that are related to the speed of the engine: this type of sound can indicate issues like a leaking exhaust manifold/header, faulty fuel injector or even a suspect VCT camshaft-phaser.

Return to the interior, and begin by checking for holes in the dash panel that look like they shouldn't be there, such as cell-phone fixings or aftermarket sat-nav mounts. Repairing the plastics of the main dash panel is almost impossible, so bear this in mind. While this may not be a 'walk away' item for some, it could be a good bargaining point.

Check the factory stereo works, listen to both a CD and a radio station

**Using a digital camera with a flash, or your mirror on-a-stick, can help you to see the condition of the body, suspension, axle, and exhaust system.**

Take a photo of the engine bay, as potentially you can use this to refer to later.

to verify the head unit works, and that there are no damaged speakers. If fitted with the Shaker 1000 audio system, the car should also have a subwoofer enclosure on the RH side of the trunk, so confirm this is present and also works.

Visually inspect the dash, headliner, console, door panels, carpets, rear trim panels and seat upholstery for damage or wear. The seat bolsters tend to wear prematurely, particularly on the driver's side, so watch out for this.

Lift the floor mats and check underneath, paying particular attention and checking for moisture on the passenger (RH) side footwell. Here, a wet carpet can indicate clogged cowl drains resulting in water coming into the car. Obviously, wet carpets can retain water and accelerate the onset of corrosion in the floors.

On convertible models, thoroughly check the condition of the hood, both inside and out; this can be very expensive to replace if damaged or worn.

Make sure the engine coolant is filled to the specified level. Check the engine oil, and, if viewing a 2005-2010 model, the hydraulic power-steering fluid.

While in the driver seat, adjust the seat position to suit you and ensure you can get comfortable. Then press the brake pedal with your right foot. The pedal should firm-up and give you a nice firm pedal feel. If the pedal goes to the floor, don't drive the car as there's probably something wrong with the brakes. On manual transmission cars depress the clutch pedal fully: you'll note it has a long action, and will likely determine your final seating position.

## Test drive

At this stage you need to either drive the car, or be driven in it. Not all Mustang owners will be willing to hand over the keys to their car for you to drive, particularly if you've never driven an American car before, or are not used to LHD. Don't push the issue; be gracious and remember that if this car was your pride and joy, you might be quite protective as well. But one consolation is that you can spend less time concentrating on actually driving, and more time on observing the driver, the inputs they're making, and also the sights, sounds and smells.

Be sure to check the vehicle is legal to be driven on the road, and that you're covered by some form of insurance. All S197 Mustangs came from the factory with three-point safety belts in the front and rear, so be sure to fasten yours before the car moves.

To start the engine, check the shifter is in park, or for manual transmission cars, that the shifter is in neutral, and you've depressed the clutch before turning the key.

The engine should crank quickly, starting cleanly and crisply, settling down after a few seconds to a smooth idle. As with most modern vehicles, when the engine is started from cold, initially, the electronic control unit (ECU) will keep the engine idling at a higher speed, and then gradually reduce the idle rpm as the engine warms up to its normal operating temperature.

If the car has an aftermarket exhaust upgrade, expect a louder and often

Check the brake/clutch fluid reservoir, and look for any evidence of leaked or spilled fluid or peeling paint. Think twice about a test drive if the fluid is low.

**Look over the whole interior for marks, wear and damage. Pay special attention to all plastics, the seat covers, and carpets. Obtaining OE replacements may be difficult in the future.**

more aggressive sound, versus the more subdued factory exhaust note. Be sure to listen out for droning at cruising speeds, which can be introduced by some aftermarket exhaust upgrades. While it may sound fantastic and be great fun on a short test drive, think about doing a long extended trip on the freeway with the same exhaust drone all the way. Also think about your neighbours and whether your local law-enforcement will likely deliver you a citation.

The key on the test drive is to listen for abnormalities, there should be no squeaks, bumps or bangs when going over mild undulations in the road. The car should track straight and not want to suddenly change direction when going over uneven surfaces, as this can indicate poor front suspension alignment. The factory suspension is competent in virtually all normal road conditions, but it's quite common for owners to swap the springs for aftermarket lowering items, for visual appeal as much as performance. Of course this looks great, but can sometimes result in a bone-jarring ride on anything but a perfect road surface.

The steering should feel tight and precise, with little free play. The factory power steering feels weighty but not heavy, while later 2011-14 cars received electric power assisted steering (EPAS) with an adjustable feel.

Larger diameter and wider wheels may enhance the kerb appeal, but sometimes they can make the ride more harsh, or increase the tendency to 'tram-line,' which is particularly apparent on rutted asphalt roads.

Test the parking brake and its ability to hold the vehicle. Before driving ensure your surroundings are safe, and be prepared in case the brake doesn't work.

On a straight clear piece of road, or in a quiet car park, be sure to test the ability of the car to slow down quickly. You're not trying to perform an emergency stop, the key thing here is to feel how the car slows, to help you gauge the condition of the braking system. Tell the owner and passengers what you plan to do, be sensible, and most importantly be safe.

The front brakes should do most of the work and the vehicle should stop cleanly, quickly, and in a straight line. There should be no vibration through the wheel or brake pedal, as this can indicate warped or overheated brake rotors. All GT models received four-channel ABS, which can be felt through the pedal if invoked.

Automatic transmissions should shift cleanly through all gears, including kickdown activated by the throttle position. Listen and feel for the engine rpm rising on shifts, this can indicate slipping and damage to the internal clutches, bands or low transmission fluid level. Listen and feel for a slipping clutch on firm acceleration with manual transmission cars, and also for clutch judder or bounce when trying to pull away smoothly. The clutch tends to engage positively, particularly on V8 powered models, and some gear noise is normal on manual transmission cars. Again, when accelerating quickly, be aware of the road conditions and your surroundings: be safe.

Keep an eye on the instruments, paying particular attention for correct operation and any warning lights. While in the seat, check the operation of all controls, lights, washers and wipers.

If you've looked at all these major points and you're still considering the car, now it's time for soul searching, further research and negotiations.

# 8 Key points
– where to look for problems

## VIN

You'll find the VIN or chassis number at the base of the windshield on the driver's side. This can give several pieces of useful information, including the specific body code, engine code and model year. Note the number down or take a photo. You can use one of the numerous free decoders available online to compare with information by the seller.

Take a photo or note down the VIN shown in the windshield, which you can either decode later, or possibly even on-the-fly via your mobile device.

## Driver's door pillar stickers

Take a photo of the information stickers attached to the B-pillar. These include the VIN and other pieces of useful information such as the wheel and tire sizes, paint code, interior trim, axle and transmission codes etc.

## Mileage

Be sure to verify the mileage shown on the digital odometer is aligned with what the seller has advertised, as this will have a direct impact on the vehicle's value.

The information stickers on the driver's door pillar can offer a host of useful information, so take a photo for later reference. Also confirm the VIN on the sticker matches the one in the windshield.

Verify the mileage shown on the digital dash. This 2013 Boss 302 shows just under 6500 miles, which tallies with the car's condition. You should make the same comparison.

## Hood leading edge

A known weak spot on earlier S197 models is the leading edge of the aluminum hood (bonnet), which can suffer from corrosion issues, so inspect this area from the top and underside.

Check the leading edge of the hood from above and below for paint blistering caused by corrosion. This hood looks fine as there's no sign of blistering.

## Wiring

Thoroughly check all visible wiring and lighting conversion work carried out, if outside of the USA or Canada. This is an important item to verify, or you could be left with a broken smart junction box (SJB) and expensive repair bills.

# 9 Serious evaluation
– 60 minutes for years of enjoyment

Score each section as follows: 4 = excellent; 3 = good; 2 = average; 1 = poor. The totting up procedure is detailed at the end of the chapter. Try to remain consistent and realistic in scoring each section.

## Exterior

All S197 Mustangs share the same foundation, and while there are numerous engineering and styling differences, the basic underpinnings remain consistent. The core of all 2005-2014 Mustangs is the steel monocoque, constructed from numerous stamped sheet-metal panels and box-sectional members, which, when spot welded together, create the bodyshell or unitised body (unibody). With no separate chassis, the bodyshell forms the structural foundation of the vehicle.

Like all vehicles constructed predominantly from steel, Mustangs have the potential to suffer from future corrosion (rust) issues, however, modern anti-corrosion treatments and paints offer superior protection. With the oldest S197 Mustang being constructed in late 2004, it's unlikely the main bodyshell will suffer from corrosion issues. However, this is not to say that issues such as accident damage or poor repair work won't be present. The condition of exterior panels, glass, paint and underlying bodyshell structure are key inspection items for your evaluation.

### Paint

4️⃣ 3️⃣ 2️⃣ 1️⃣

Chapter 14 is dedicated to paintwork imperfections and their implication, but it's important to realize that paint and bodywork are likely to be major bargaining areas. Be thorough with your assessment, and look closely at panel edges, door shuts, window rubbers, seals and plastic trim. These are all tell-tale areas that can show if the vehicle was not fully disassembled when painted. This can also indicate a hidden past, like previous collision or accident damage.

Look closely for damage to the paint finish, like stone chips and scratches; it often helps to view a car under artificial light or in bright daylight to really see the quality of the paint finish. You should try to avoid viewing a car in the rain or while it's wet, as this can hide many imperfections or issues.

It's important to understand that correcting issues with paintwork can require many hours of preparation, painting and polishing, so refinishing a vehicle to a high standard is not a cheap exercise, and is best avoided.

From a side-on view, check the alignment and trueness of the panels and character lines. Viewing in good light shows reflections, and highlights imperfections.

### Panels

4️⃣ 3️⃣ 2️⃣ 1️⃣

The key horizontal character line between the front fender, door panel and rear quarter panel should line up perfectly, as should

**Looking from the rear, check for square and even panels with consistent gaps. The paint on this GT really shows the owner cares for it.**

Look at the car head-on, check for even panel gaps, symmetry and character lines. This 2005 GT looks nice and straight.

From the rear, this GT shows off the characteristic tri-bar tail-lights. The silver stripes and black paint really give this car a great look. Note the aftermarket exhaust mufflers.

the lower character lines on the doors and rear fenders that make up the simulated scoop, which is synonymous with Mustang.

Check closely for dents, dings or other paint damage to the doors, front and rear fenders, hood, roof and trunk lid. Issues here, left unchecked, can mean the premature onset of corrosion. The doors are a pillarless design, with only the glass and solidly mounted rear-view mirror housings extending above the door belt line. Be sure to check the outer edges for car park damage or chips.

Upon opening the trunk, check the drain gullies around the opening and near the hinges, as these areas can hold water and debris if the car is not cleaned regularly. Check for evidence of poor masking or overspray in these areas, as well as in the door jambs, which can point to a hidden past.

Check the door edges for minor paint chips or car-park damage. The small paint chip seen here could result in corrosion.

Closely check the front bumper facia for any impact damage, deformation, paint issues or evidence of overspray. Look for good fitment and color match between the fenders, hood and facia. A mismatch in color, or evidence of overspray, could highlight previous replacement or repair. The same applies to the rear bumper facia, which is a large, one-piece item that wraps around the lower rear portion of the car. Again, color match is important, and check for marks, scuffs, evidence of overspray, and maybe even deformation of the plastics which may have been caused by previous parking indiscretions.

Check for damage on the side skirts (rocker mouldings), which may show scars from off-road excursions.

The trunk in an S197 Mustang can hold plenty of luggage or groceries. Check the trunk lid and edges for corrosion or damage.

Be sure to inspect the leading edge and underside of the aluminum hood. This is a known weak spot for corrosion, caused by particle contamination under the paint from the factory in earlier S197 models, which can result in unsightly blisters and peeling if left unchecked.

Check for overspray and the onset of rust on the underside of the doors, particularly if the drainholes in the metal

Check around the trunk hinges and drain gullies for evidence of overspray. This area can also accumulate dirt and grime, so check for the onset of corrosion.

appear blocked. Water that finds its way inside the doors will accumulate at the bottom, and could cause the bottom and outer skin to rust from the inside out.

Look closely at the rocker (sill) covers (side skirts) for any damage or marks.

Note the two small marks on this rear bumper cover

Look over the front bumper cover for any stone chips, marks or deformation of the plastics. Ensure you check low down and underneath, as these areas can be easily overlooked.

Check the rear lower quarters of the bumper facia for paint damage caused by the tire flicking debris from the road surface. This Boss 302 has spats which help to prevent this.

## Shut lines
[4] [3] [2] [1]

The panel gaps and shut lines can be a good reference point when looking for evidence of previous damage or repairs.

The underside of this black hood is showing signs of the typical corrosion problems found on early S197 models.

The factory has strict tolerances that would have to be adhered to, so unevenness or asymmetry here could help to identify problems.

## Exterior trim
[4] [3] [2] [1]

There's little exterior trim or brightwork, but some models were fitted with vinyl decals and stripes that can be easily overlooked when viewing. The Shelby GT500 and Boss 302 models both have specially produced stripes and decals, which are important styling features. Any decals should be inspected for damage, tearing, fading or deterioration, as replacing them could be more expensive than you think.

## Wipers
[4] [3] [2] [1]

On all models check the wiper arms are aligned and the blades park in the correct position. Be sure to fully check their operation when in the vehicle, as these will likely feature on the annual safety check. When replacing blades it's important to buy high-quality items, as cheaper alternatives may have an annoying squeak.

## Convertible top
[4] [3] [2] [1]

Test the operation of the folding roof mechanism thoroughly. Service parts are available for the actuation system, but it's an expense best avoided. Closely check the condition of the fabric, especially on edges, corners and where the roof folds up for stowage. Any problems here can be expensive to repair, and fitting a new convertible roof is not to be taken

Check around the front door hinges for overspray, which could be evidence of previous accident repairs.

A photo like this can confirm the presence of the door seal or the onset of corrosion.

Look at the panel gaps, body lines, decals, and overall view of the car. This 2010 Shelby GT500 convertible looks nice, but try to avoid viewing a car in the rain like this if possible.

The reflective hockey stick stripes are key styling elements on this 2013 Boss 302.

lightly. On models with light-colored roofs, check closely for marks or ingrained dirt that may be difficult to remove/clean.

## Glass

While the condition of the glass might not seem important, shipping large pieces of glass around the world is not cheap. If you live outside of the United States or Canada, be sure to look closely at the glass. Pay particular attention to the windshield within the sweep of the wipers for stone chips and other damage, as this area may come under scrutiny during the annual roadworthiness test. Check for vertical scratches on the door glass, which can be caused by dirt or grit getting lodged in the doorbelt seals, and scraped against the glass as windows are opened and closed.

This 2010 Shelby GT500 has both rocker and LeMans stripes that run the length of the car. Pay close attention to the vinyl. (Courtesy Ray Welch)

## Lights

Check the operation of all exterior lights. If you're outside of the USA or Canada, ensure the lighting is configured correctly to be legal within your country. A little homework to understand the requirements is a good idea before you view the car, as wiring conversions can be expensive if you don't have the necessary skills or tools to make the amendments required.

As these cars use an SJB, or smart junction box, to control the lighting and electrical circuits of the vehicle, it's very important that any conversion work has been done correctly, and should ideally be documented with receipts

Take a look at the wiper arms, blades and windshield within the sweep for marks, stone chips or other damage. Test washers and wipers while driving.

Check the convertible top for damage. This 2005 GT looks in great condition.

Check the operation of all lights. The tail-lights on this Shelby have been converted to meet UK lighting regulations. (Courtesy Ray Welch)

or invoices. If you encounter issues when testing the lighting circuits, or have directional indicators that flash too fast, investigate further!

## Wheels & tires
### Tire condition/rating  [4] [3] [2] [1]

Check the tire sizes, and compare to the sticker in the driver's door jamb. Obviously if aftermarket wheels are fitted it's likely this information is incorrect, but you should verify the tire speed rating is suitable for the vehicle. All Mustang GTs were shod with high-performance tires with a 'Z' speed rating (over 149mph). The Boss 302 and Shelby models received specific high-performance compound tires, which can be expensive items to replace, so you should consider this when viewing one of these desirable ponies.

This attractive 20in Shelby Razor wheel has a raw machined aluminum rim, which will corrode if not well looked after.

Ensure there's plenty of available tread depth, and look for excessive wear on the inside or outside edges of the tires, which can be an indication of poor alignment. Look for evidence of rubbing, particularly if wide aftermarket wheels have been installed.

### Wheel condition  [4] [3] [2] [1]

Whether they are factory aluminum wheels or aftermarket versions, check thoroughly for curb damage and paint or other finish defects. Refurbishing aluminum wheels can be expensive, so it's best avoided, particularly if the wheels have a machined, polished or plated finish.

Forged 19 x 9.5in wheels and Goodyear Eagle F1 tires adorn the front of 2013/14 Shelby GT500 models.

### Hub bearings & steering joints  [4] [3] [2] [1]

It's important to check the condition and security of all ball joints, links and gaiters within the steering assembly, as problems here can be costly if a new rack assembly is required. Unfortunately, it's difficult to check the wheel or hub bearings for excessive play without lifting or jacking the front wheels.

## Interior
### Seats  [4] [3] [2] [1]

All 2005-2014 models were fitted with front bucket seats, featuring separate height adjustable head-rests. The covers are trimmed in complementary colors to the rest of the interior, either in cloth or leather. The standard seats are comfortable and offer plenty of adjustment. Some models received electrically adjustable driver's seats and optional seat heaters.

It's also worth noting that the front seats contain airbags, which deploy in the event of a side impact. These were initially optional items, but were incorporated as a standard feature on all models from 2008 onwards.

In 2012, Ford added race-inspired Recaro seats to the options list for Boss

Left: Parchment seat covers, carpets and lower dash panels work together nicely.
Center: The charcoal interior contrasts well with the silver dash applique.
Right: the medium grey interior complements the silver paint on this 2005 GT.

302 and Shelby GT500 models. For 2013/14, the Recaro seats were also made available on GT models, as part of the 'GT track package' option.

One area to pay particular attention to is the upper lateral seat bolsters, which can show signs of wear where occupants lean on this part of the seat to help themselves out of the car. Replacement seat covers are available, but this could be used in your favour as a bargaining chip.

## Carpets
Factory carpets are complementary in color to the rest of the interior. Check for wear, ground in dirt, cigarette burns or other marks that will be hard to remove.

## Headlining
The headliner is an important area to check within the interior as although replacements may be available, fitting them can be awkward and labour intensive. Check the material finish is not marked or damaged and is the correct complementary color to the interior seats, door cards and other trim items.

## Door cards & interior panels
All 2005-2014 Mustangs have large one-piece moulded plastic door cards in either black, grey or parchment colors to complement the interior trim. The door cards have a leather grain pattern with a leather/vinyl or cloth insert, usually in either a contrasting color or design. This gives the door panels a retro look, which is reminiscent of the original 1960s design.

Check for scratches, cracks or damage to all plastics, as this can be hard to repair, and replacement is often simpler. The door panels also house the front

Left: The vibrant red and charcoal interior looks great on this black GT.
Center: The high-back Recaro seats are a popular option with enthusiasts.
Right: 2013/14 Shelby GT500 leather Recaro seats with the Cobra emblem.

speakers for the audio system, the door handles, and the power window switches.

### Door locks [4] [3] [2] [1]
All models received remote central locking, with manual override switches on the inside. The door locks can be operated with wireless remote or the ignition key.

The power locks, or more accurately the latch mechanisms, work in unison with the power windows. When the latch is released, an electrical signal is sent to the power windows to slightly lower the glass out of the window channel, so it does not prevent the door from opening.

Above: A 2005 GT Premium with charcoal interior and door panels. Right: V6 models with parchment and medium grey door panels.

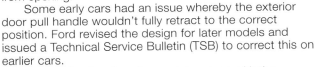

Some early cars had an issue whereby the exterior door pull handle wouldn't fully retract to the correct position. Ford revised the design for later models and issued a Technical Service Bulletin (TSB) to correct this on earlier cars.

The interior door handles work in unison with the aforementioned latch and door pins to open the door, and lower the window from the upper seals.

The attractive 2005 'interior color accent package' included corresponding seats and door cards trimmed in red leather.

### Window winders [4] [3] [2] [1]
Check for smooth and correct operation of the mechanisms and switches. All S197 Mustangs have soft-close power windows, which learn the fully open and closed positions to gently stop, rather than thump, into the door stops or upper seals.

### Steering wheel [4] [3] [2] [1]
All 2005-2009 Mustangs received a sporty black three-spoke steering wheel with mandatory driver's airbag and tri-bar pony emblem in the center. V6 and GT models with the 'Sport appearance package' or 'Interior upgrade package' got a leather-wrapped wheel and satin aluminum spokes. The horn push and cruise control functions are built into the wheel.

The premium wheel was revised in 2010, but still retained a similar three-spoke design, sporting silver accents

All 2005-14 Mustangs had power windows with switches built into the doors. as in this 2013 model.

Exterior door handles were all painted body color, with locks manually operated by key or wireless remote. Interior handles came in either black plastic or aluminum. Note the manual door lock override switch.

**Steering wheel variations, top, left-right: Leather wrapped 2005-2009 Mustang GT wheel; standard 2005-2009 wheel; leather wrapped Shelby GT500 wheel (GT500KR shown); 2010-2014 standard wheel with the running pony center emblem; bottom, left: The 2010-2014 Mustang GT received a leather wrapped wheel (Alcantara wrapped Boss 302 wheel shown).**

and additional multi-function controls. The tri-bar pony was replaced with a polished running pony emblem.

2007-2009 Shelby GT500 models received a unique all black leather wrapped wheel featuring the coiled cobra snake emblem in the center. From 2010 the Shelby and Boss 302 models had the same wheel as other models, but wrapped in Alcantara with the corresponding cobra or running pony emblem.

### Instrument panel & dashboard

The dash panel is a key component of the interior that is difficult to replace, so look out for poorly executed aftermarket stereo installations, holes drilled into the plastics and other damage as this will likely be impossible to repair.

The gauges and instrument cluster are fully electronic, with the movements and warning lamps being controlled by various sensor inputs and signals. Check for correct operation of all gauges, and be wary if any are not working. The popular MyColor dash allows drivers to select their preferred instrument panel color, but in reality this is often set once and never touched again. Turn the headlamps on to check that the dash and console lights also come on.

### Trunk interior

If the trunk lid seal isn't doing a very good job of keeping the weather out, there could be rust beginning to develop on the trunk floor. Remove or lift the mat to have a peek underneath.

On models with the optional Shaker 1000 stereo system the subwoofer will be installed on the passenger side. Check the enclosure hasn't been damaged by heavy items rolling around in the trunk

### Spare wheel & tool kit

Check the spare and its condition, if the tire has insufficient tread, or has perished this could fail the annual safety inspection. While not a big fault, it could be bargaining point.

**Models with the optional Shaker 1000 stereo system have a subwoofer in the trunk.**

Lift the trunk mat to look at the condition of the floor. The rear shock absorber upper mounts are found in the trunk as shown.

Not all models were equipped with a spare wheel and jack from the factory, which is worth noting, as it might be sensible to consider taking out breakdown or tow cover from a reputable company.

Take a look at the spare tire and wheel well. This Mustang Boss 302 didn't come with a spare wheel.

## Mechanicals & under the hood

Fortunately, given the age of S197 Mustangs, it's unlikely you'll encounter too many with replacement engines or mismatched parts. But this doesn't mean you won't, as these vehicles get older and are passed through the hands of different owners.

Don't be afraid to compare what's in front of you with reference material from magazines, books and other sources. It's relatively easy to find the original Ford sales brochures, owner's manuals and VIN decoding tools on the internet, to help you determine if the car is genuinely represented, with the correct parts and options.

### General impression
⁴ ³ ² ¹

The key thing to consider in the engine bay is the overall condition and level of cleanliness. Some owners may have chosen to customise, change and replace components, to 'dress up' or modify their engine for greater performance. Consider the potential increase in insurance premiums, and whether you can find replacement parts or service items. Ask the seller for any paperwork or documentation relating to modifications or upgrades; ideally they will have receipts and invoices.

### VIN or chassis number
⁴ ³ ² ¹

Writing down or taking a photo of the VIN could be important to help you identify the original build specification of the car. The VIN is visible at the base of the windshield or on the driver's door pillar data label. Here is an example –

| Vehicle Identification Number (VIN) | | |
|---|---|---|
| **VIN – 1ZVBP8CUXD5269422** | | |
| 1ZV | Manufacturer | Automotive Alliance International – Ford passenger car |
| B | Restraint system type | Manual belts with driver and passenger frontal air bags and side inflatable restraints |
| P8C | Line, Series, Body code | Coupe, 2-Door Sedan |
| U | Engine Type | 5.0L DOHC 4V, V8, Gasoline, Ford, 444hp (Boss 302) |
| X | Check Digit | 0-9 or X |
| D | Model Year | 2013 |
| 5 | Assembly Plant | Flat Rock Assembly Plant (AAI): Flat Rock, Michigan |
| 269422 | Production Sequence Number | 269422 (Ford Division) |

## Bodywork

Within the engine bay, all body structure components like the firewall, inner fenders and front cross-member are painted body color from the factory. The underside of the hood should have its black sound-deadening mat. Check for evidence of paint overspray down the edges of the inner fenders, firewall and other components within the engine bay, as this could indicate previous damage or body repairs.

**Check inner fenders and strut towers on both sides for evidence of overspray, which results if not properly masked or disassembled when repairs are done.**

## Wiring & electrical system

Pay special attention to the condition of the wiring and looms, if there are lots of joins, splices and wires that look like they're out of place, they probably shouldn't be there. Be suspicious of poorly fitted electrical accessories, try to investigate further. Wiring can be problematic and expensive to repair; electrical systems are probably the least understood component of a car, and Mustangs are no different.

Lighting conversions should be closely examined, as incorrect wiring or installation can result in costly damage to the SJB. Check in the boot/trunk, where the wiring to the tail and reversing lights will be changed to meet regulations in other countries. Remove the plastic rear tail-lamp covers, and check for splices and joins to the wiring harness.

## Charging system

All models have a warning light, which illuminates if the battery is not charging with the engine running. With the engine idling, listen for the tell-tale rattle that can indicate the alternator bearings are showing signs of wear.

## Battery

Installed on a purpose built mounting and secured with a hold-down strap, the battery is easily accessible. It's important to install the correct battery with the recommended ratings, or reliability issues can result, particularly in colder climates.

If the battery has been disconnected there are several systems that must either be reset or go through a relearn cycle. This includes the aforementioned electric soft-close windows, the engine idle trim settings, and transmission adaptive shift parameters, in addition to the more obvious clock and radio station presets.

**Check the battery is properly secured on its mount and the terminals are free from corrosion. This is a 2013 model: earlier models had terminals the other way around.**

## Radiator & fans

The radiator is usually trouble-free, provided the correct engine coolant and servicing intervals have been adhered to. It's a known problem that some radiator/coolant recovery tank pressure caps fail to seal, and are unable to hold the required pressure; evidence of staining may be seen on the top of the tank if this is the case.

Check the coolant level, and all hoses for signs of perishing or mechanical contact/rubbing.

All cars were equipped with electric cooling fans from the factory, governed by the Powertrain Control Module (PCM). It's difficult to verify correct operation with the engine cold, or air-conditioning switch off, so if possible leave the engine running following the test drive to check the fans come on.

### Hoses

4 3 2 1

Check the condition of all rubber hoses, particularly those used within the fuel system. Check for perishing, cracking or incorrect specification, as standard water hose is not suitable for fuel or oil.

### Brake master cylinder

4 3 2 1

Check the brake fluid level and look around the master cylinder for evidence of leaked or spilled fluid. If any fluid is present around the unions or under the reservoir, don't drive the car as it could be dangerous. Brake fluid can harm paintwork, so this may also be a good tell-tale sign if the fluid has leaked.

When you press on the brake pedal, there should be a firm pedal feel. If it goes to the floor, don't drive the car.

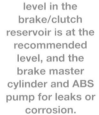

### Brake servo

4 3 2 1

Power assisted brakes, by the means of a vacuum servo or 'booster' are standard equipment on all S197 Mustangs. If the servo is not functioning correctly the brake pedal will feel heavy, and require far greater pedal effort to stop the vehicle.

### Clutch master cylinder (manual trans.)

4 3 2 1

The master cylinder shares the same hydraulic fluid reservoir as the braking system, so check for leaks here at the same time as the brake master cylinder. The best way to gauge operation is by depressing the clutch pedal while in the driver's seat. You

Check the fluid level in the brake/clutch reservoir is at the recommended level, and the brake master cylinder and ABS pump for leaks or corrosion.

should feel firm resistance on the pedal and when at rest. A spongy pedal or one with little resistance may suggest there's a problem with the clutch hydraulic system.

### Washer system

4 3 2 1

The windscreen washer reservoir is mounted below the right hand inner fender, with the washer jets mounted on the hood. Check for an even spray pattern across the windshield, and correct wash-wipe operation.

### Engine identification

4 3 2 1

The base engine for 2005-2010 was the 4.0L (221ci) 'Cologne' V6 which features a SOHC (single over-head camshaft) design with an iron-block and aluminum cylinder heads. This entry level engine option delivers a smooth, dependable 210hp and 240lb/ft, perfect for highway cruising and daily driver duties.

For 2005-2010 the Mustang GT received the all aluminum 4.6L (281ci) 3V V8. Featuring a SOHC design with variable camshaft timing (VCT) and three valve per cylinder (3V), this engine produces a solid 300hp and 320lb/ft of torque. Later

The 4.0L SOHC 'Cologne' V6 served as the base engine from 2005-2010, producing 210hp and 240lb/ft of torque.

Alongside the V8 in 2011, the 3.7L 'Duratec' V6 features a modern 24-valve DOHC valvetrain with Ti-VCT, and produces a fuel efficient 305hp and 280lb/ft of torque.

revised in 2010 to produce 315hp and 325lb/ft, this engine is commonly referred to as the Modular 4.6L 3V V8 by Ford enthusiasts.

The aging base model SOHC V6 was replaced in 2011 with the all aluminum 3.7L DOHC 24-valve Duratec V6 which is some 40lbs (18kg) lighter. Featuring the latest Ti-VCT (Twin-independent Variable Camshaft Timing) technology this engine has a factory rating of 305hp and 280lb/ft of torque.

Also for 2011 the Mustang GT received an all-new 5.0L (302ci) 32-valve V8 engine. Based on the Ford Modular engine platform the 'Coyote' V8 features a 4-valve (4V) cylinder head design with DOHC and Ti-VCT. For 2011-12, the 'Coyote' boasted an impressive factory rating of 412hp and 390lb/ft of torque, which was further increased to 420hp and 390lb/ft for 2013-14.

A special variant of the 'Coyote' V8 was developed under the Ford codename 'Road-Runner,' specifically for the 2012/13 Mustang Boss 302. Producing 444hp and 380lb/ft of torque, the purpose built high-revving normally aspirated V8 paid homage to the original 1969 and 1970 Boss 302 cars that Ford built to win the SCCA Trans-Am racing series.

The 2007-2010 Shelby GT500 featured a supercharged 5.4L (330ci) Modular V8 codenamed 'Condor,' derived from the Ford GT supercar, which is commonly referred to as the Modular 5.4L 4V. With an iron engine block, aluminum DOHC 4V cylinder heads and positive displacement supercharger, the 2007-2009 Shelby GT500 produced a potent 500hp and 480lb/ft of torque, which was later increased to 540hp and 500lb/ft of torque for 2010.

The 5.4L 4V engine saw several engineering enhancements for the 2011/12 GT500, including a switch to a lighter aluminum engine block, saving 102lbs (46kg) over previous models. All of the combined changes increased output to 550hp and 510lb/ft of torque.

The 2013-14 Shelby GT500 features the most powerful production V8 ever built by Ford. A highly re-engineered derivative of the 5.4L 4V engine, the 'Trinity' V8 utilises an

The 4.6L 3V SOHC Modular V8 was the motivation for all 2005-2010 Mustang GT models, and features Variable Camshaft Timing.

The 5.0L 4V Ti-VCT V8 or 'Coyote,' introduced in 2011 with 412hp, was an instant hit. The factory rating was increased in 2013/14 to 420hp.

This is the high-revving 444hp 'Road Runner' 5.0L (302ci) V8, specially developed for the Mustang Boss 302, and proven on the track.

Derived from the Ford GT supercar, the Supercharged 5.4L 4V DOHC Modular V8 is both robust and powerful. This is the 540hp Shelby GT500KR version. (Courtesy Alex Fearn)

The pinnacle of S197 Mustang performance is the 2013/14 Shelby GT500, with supercharged 5.8L 4V modular V8 producing 662hp, and 631lb/ft of torque.

application specific engine block with a greater 5.8L (355ci) displacement and a 2.3L TVS Supercharger to produce an astonishing factory rating of 662hp and 631lb/ft of torque.

All engines are reliable, and offer trouble-free motoring if serviced regularly. When viewing a car, use online references to compare with other examples of the same model, which can identify any potential problems.

### Engine leaks

Check for evidence of fluid leaks, but you shouldn't find any visible signs if the vehicle is well maintained, as these modern engines don't tend to leak.

### Engine mountings

These items are normally fairly robust and generally only need replacement if the rubber insulators are worn.

### Intake manifold

All engine variants feature intake manifolds fashioned from lightweight composite materials, and have tuned plenum and runner lengths to deliver optimum performance within the engine's operating range. The 4.6L 3V V8 also utilises charge motion control valves (CMCV), which are butterfly valves within the intake tract that can increase turbulence at lower engine speeds and improve torque.

The 2012/2013 Boss 302 models were fitted with a unique composite inlet manifold with shorter intake runners suited towards high-rpm performance. Shelby GT500 models equipped with 5.4L and 5.8L engines have unique intake systems specifically designed to cater for the supercharger and associated intercooler.

### Fuel injection system

All S197 Mustangs have a highly efficient electronically controlled sequential fuel injection system which tightly controls fuel consumption and emissions. The fuel system utilises a high-pressure in-tank fuel pump to supply the fuel rails and injectors. The Powertrain Control Module (PCM) automatically adjusts the fuelling, ignition and camshaft timing (on models so equipped), for maximum efficiency and performance in all conditions.

These highly reliable systems usually require only regular routine maintenance and fuel filter changes to keep them operating in peak condition.

### Ignition system

Controlled directly by the Powertrain Control Module (PCM), the ignition timing is automatically adjusted according to various factors, such as engine load, throttle position and fuel quality. Camshaft and crankshaft position sensors are used to read the engine speed and rotational position. The PCM sends low-voltage control signals to the ignition coils, to fire the sparkplug at the optimal time in the combustion cycle for maximum efficiency.

The 4.0L V6 engine utilises a single ignition coil-pack with high-tension leads connected to each individual sparkplug. The later multi-valve 3.7L V6 and V8 engines utilize coil-on-plug (COP) with one ignition coil per cylinder.

The 4.6L 3V V8 engines are known to suffer from carbon build-up on the sparkplugs after several thousand miles of service, which can result in them sticking within the cylinder head, so extra care is required when performing a sparkplug change.

### Exhaust manifolds & downpipes
All 2005-2014 Mustangs left the factory with cast iron exhaust manifolds, except for the 2011-on GT and 2012/13 Boss 302, which both benefit from stainless steel headers. The exhaust downpipes house the catalytic convertors and oxygen sensors, routing the spent exhaust gases rearwards down the middle of the car to the H-pipe and then up over the axle to the rear mufflers and tailpipes.

### Steering rack
All S197 Mustangs have a rack and pinion steering assembly, which is either hydraulically or electrically assisted. There should be no perceivable free play in the steering; be wary as replacement steering racks are available, but expensive.

### Power steering pump/reservoir

Models fitted with hydraulic power assisted steering (PAS) systems from the factory utilize an hydraulic pump driven via the engine crankshaft, be sure to check the pump and associated pipework for any evidence of fluid leaks.

### AC compressor
Check the belt-driven factory air-conditioning compressor for obvious leaks and any damage to the associated pipes and hoses. Verify the air-conditioning blows cool air on the test drive, as repairing, replacing and recharging the system can be expensive.

### Front suspension

All 2005-2014 Mustangs share the same MacPherson strut front suspension system, utilizing reverse-L lower control arms and stabilizer (anti-roll) bar.

The tubular stabilizer bar plays a key role in how the car handles, so it's important to check the security of the end-links and bushings. The lower control arms are anchored to the front subframe (or K-member) via two large bushes; and to the strut assembly via a ball joint. It's difficult to check if these need replacement without access to a lift or special tools, so in some cases a visual inspection has to suffice.

Popular upgrades include replacing the factory springs with aftermarket versions which lower the ride-height, for a sportier appearance and handling. Similarly, the struts and stabilizer bars can also be swapped out for upgraded or adjustable units. Ford Racing, Steeda, Roush and other vendors offer bespoke kits, which are tailored to improve handling or drag-strip performance.

## Brakes
### Front brakes

The same basic front braking system was fitted to all 2005-2010 Mustangs from the factory, utilizing aluminum two-piston floating calipers and either 11.5in (290mm) rotors/discs on V6 models or 12.4in (315mm) rotors/discs for V8 GT models.

In line with the more powerful engines for 2011, the standard brakes were

The front-strut assembly and the standard two-piston aluminum brake calipers and ventilated rotors/discs.

The optional high-performance Brembo 4-piston calipers and 14in (355mm) vented rotors available on 2011-on GT models.

upgraded to larger diameter 12.4in (315mm) discs on V6 models. GT models received larger 13.2in (335mm) versions, while both retained the same basic two-piston caliper design.

At the same time a new high-performance brake option was introduced for 2011 GT models, offering larger Brembo 4-piston fixed aluminum calipers and 14in (355mm) ventilated discs, providing better pedal feel and fade resistance when pushed.

All 2007-2012 Shelby GT500 and 2012/13 Boss 302 models received the high-performance Brembo front brakes, but with different pad compounds to suit each application. The 2013/14 Shelby GT500 received even larger Brembo 6-piston calipers, and gargantuan 15in (380mm) rotors/discs to counter the 662hp available from the 5.8L supercharged engine.

If well maintained with OEM or quality replacement parts, all systems offer excellent service under normal conditions.

## Rear brakes

All S197 Mustangs received aluminum single piston calipers that feature an integral parking brake mechanism. Mostly cars received 11.8in (300mm) rear ventilated rotors, except for the 2013/14 Shelby GT500 which got larger 13.8in (350mm) rotors.

If well maintained, the factory brakes are highly effective, but some owners choose to swap the brake rotors for drilled/slotted versions, as much for looks as improved performance.

## Handbrake/parking brake

Actuated by a lever on the driver side of the transmission tunnel, the parking brake can feel a little awkward to operate on 2005-2009 Mustangs, but was revised for later models. The cable assemblies pull a lever on the rear brake calipers, which mechanically pushes the pads against the disc or rotor. The rubber boot on the end of the cables should be inspected; if perished or missing this could permit water into the cable assemblies causing the steel wire core to rust and expand, resulting in a seized and non-functional parking brake.

Single-piston rear calipers and 11.8in (300mm) rotors were fitted to all models, except the 2013/14 Shelby GT500 which received larger 13.8in (350mm) rotors.

## Gearbox/transmission

5- & 6-speed manual

Four different manual transmissions were used between 2005 and 2014. V6 powered 2005-2010 cars received the proven Tremec T5 5-speed, while all V8 GT models received the beefier Tremec TR-3650 5-speed. While both are stout and reliable, the TR-3650 is known to be a little noisy in normal operation.

From 2011 onwards, production swapped to the jointly developed Ford/Getrag

MT82 6-speed manual transmission, paired with the more powerful engines introduced at the same time. The MT-82 is smoother and quieter in operation than its predecessors, although early variants suffered with poor shift quality, which Ford rectified by changing the fluid specification. The MT82 was fitted to all models from 2011, except the Shelby GT500.

The brutish power of the Shelby GT500 required the use of a tougher transmission, so all 2007-2014 models received the Tremec TR-6060 6-speed manual transmission to handle the additional torque produced by the supercharged engine.

2005-2010 V6 = Tremec T5 5-speed manual transmission
2005-2010 GT = Tremec TR-3650 5-speed manual transmission
2011-2014 V6 & GT = Ford/Getrag MT-82 6-speed manual transmission
2007-2014 Shelby GT500 = Tremec TR-6060 6-speed manual transmission

With all manual transmissions, check for smooth but positive engagement of gears. Stubborn, notchy shifts can indicate wear to the synchronisers.

Some people choose to replace the factory remote shifter with aftermarket versions for more precise control. While this can give a racy feel, it does lessen the refinement, making shifting feel more agricultural, which can get tiresome on a daily commute.

### 5- & 6-speed automatic  ④ ③ ② ①

The 2005 Mustang saw the introduction of the 5-speed 5R55S electronically controlled automatic transmission, which is highly acclaimed as being a robust and reliable unit. Both V6 and V8 models received the same transmissions, regardless of axle ratios or other options.

Again, the engineering changes in 2011 saw the introduction of the new 6-speed 6R80 Automatic transmission to be paired with the new engines. The additional gear helps to further improve fuel economy and boost performance.

2005-2010 V6 & GT = 5R55S 5-speed automatic
2011-2014 V6 & GT = 6R80 6-speed automatic

Listen for engine speed rising on shifts, which can indicate slipping and wear to the transmission internals. There is no transmission fluid dipstick, so you may not be able to check the color, or smell the fluid to gauge its condition. Being electronically controlled, they need to learn or relearn their shift calibration if the battery is disconnected, so if the car you're viewing is not a daily driver, then be aware that shifts during the relearn process after reconnecting the battery can be more harsh than in normal operation.

**The TR-6060 transmission, exhaust and heat shielding. Note the plastic cover protecting the fuel filter and pipes on the left chassis rail. (Courtesy Alex Fearn)**

### Rear axle  ④ ③ ② ①

All V6 Mustangs between 2005 and 2010 were fitted with the tried and trusted 7.5in ring and pinion gears with 28-spline axles. All featured 3.31 axle ratio and a conventional (open) differential assembly.

All V8 models received the larger and more rugged 8.8in ring and pinion assembly, paired with heavy duty 31-spline rear axles and fitted with a Traction-Lok clutch type-limited slip differential. 2005-2006 manual transmission cars received 3.55 ratio gears, while those with automatic transmissions all received 3.31 ratio gears. In 2007 the standard axle ratio for all V8 equipped models (including Shelby GT500) was revised to 3.31, with the 3.55 ratio only being available as a factory option on manual transmission cars.

The limited edition 2008-2009 'Bullitt' Mustangs all featured a manual transmission and higher ratio 3.73 gears for improved acceleration.

For 2010 the standard V8 GT axle ratio remained 3.31, with optional 3.55 and 3.73 gears available on cars equipped with manual transmissions from the factory, while the Shelby GT500 received higher ratio 3.55 gears.

Starting in 2011, all models received an 8.8in Traction-Lok limited slip differential as standard, replacing the older and weaker 7.5in conventional units entirely. The new Duratec V6 powered models were fitted with economy conscious 2.73 ratio gears, while only V6 coupe models with manual transmissions had the option of the higher 3.31 ratio. The standard ratio axle for the new 5.0L Coyote V8 powered GT models was 3.31, with optional 3.55 and 3.73 ratios available on manual transmission cars only. The 2011-2012 V8 GT models fitted with the optional 6-speed automatic transmission also had the option to select a 3.15 ratio axle in favour of greater economy, but this choice was later dropped for 2013.

The 2011-2012 Shelby GT500 was equipped with 3.55 gears as standard, with the optional higher ratio 3.73 gears fitted when the SVT Performance Package was selected.

The track-focused 2012-2013 Boss 302 Laguna Seca models all received a 3.73 ratio axle with a high-performance Torsen helical differential. Regular Boss 302 models received the same 3.73 gears with a standard clutch type Traction-Lok differential, the Torsen unit being available as an option. The 2013-2014 GT models could also have the Torsen equipped axle if the GT Track Package option was selected.

For 2013-2014 the Shelby GT500 received taller 3.31 rear gears, with the option of also adding the Torsen helical limited slip differential as part of the revised SVT Performance Package, which could be further augmented with a differential oil cooler and pump with the SVT Track Pack option.

The rear axles from the factory were not painted, except for those on the 2012-2013 Boss 302 models and 2013-2014 Shelby GT500, so surface rust may be expected.

Axle codes can be found on the door sticker and axle tags, which can be used to verify the gear ratio.

As with all differentials, check for excessive gear noise or whine on acceleration and when coasting. This can indicate a worn crown-wheel and pinion. The Torsen differential can be heard in operation at lower speeds, sometimes as a gentle thud when going from coast to drive.

It's important to use the correct gear oil grade in all axles, and using the recommended additives is especially important with clutch-type Traction-Lok units.

### Rear suspension

All S197 Mustangs share the same basic 3-link solid axle rear suspension configuration. The two lower control arms and upper central link anchor the axle and control the driving and rotational forces, while the additional Panhard rod helps to control lateral movement and cornering forces. Coil springs; jounce bumpers and telescopic shock absorbers control the compliance and damping, while the solid stabilizer (anti-roll) bar helps keep body roll in check.

All links utilize rubber bushings, and should be checked as part of any routine safety inspection or maintenance. The lower control arm bushings are a key point, as these transmit the driving forces to the body and take a lot of punishment. Some owners choose to fit stronger aftermarket tubular or billet lower control arms often with polyurethane bushings, and feel that replacing the factory rubber bushings with polyurethane helps to tighten up the rear end. However, while they usually lasts longer than rubber, these stiffer bushings can make the ride feel too harsh.

Check for fluid leaks from the tubular shock absorbers, which will require immediate replacement if leaking.

## Test drive (not less than 15 minutes)

If possible try to start the car from cold, however, you may find that the owner has tested the vehicle before your arrival and therefore this is not possible. The engine should fire with zero fuss, and immediately all warning indicators within the instrument cluster should go out, except for the parking brake warning. The engine initially will idle high, but will gradually slow after around 10-15 seconds to a smooth idle under the guidance of the PCM. All models will usually reach full operating temperature within a few miles. Test the heater, air-con, stereo, seat heaters, power mirrors and windows, and any other features while in the car. It'll only take a few seconds for each one.

If the owner allows you to drive (insurance permitting of course) your primary concern should be safety and consideration for other road users. Secondly you should be considerate towards the owner's pride and joy.

There should be no squeaks, bumps or bangs when going over mild bumps or undulations in the road. The car should track straight and should not want to suddenly change direction when going over uneven surfaces, as this can indicate poor front suspension alignment or worse. If the steering feels vague this can indicate wear in the steering rack, which can be expensive to fix. Factory power steering (either hydraulically or electrically assisted) feels weighty but not heavy, but this doesn't affect parking.

On a straight clear piece of road with no one behind you, or in a quiet parking lot, test the ability of the car to slow down rapidly. Tell the owner and passengers what you plan to do, be sensible and most importantly be safe. You're not trying to perform an emergency stop, nor forcibly activate the ABS or AdvanceTrac stability system, the key thing is to feel how the car slows while gauging feedback though the steering wheel and pedal, which can greatly help to gauge the condition of the braking system. The front brakes should do most of the work and the vehicle should stop cleanly, quickly and in a straight line. No vibration should be felt through the wheel or brake pedal as this can indicate warped rotors.

A ramp check is highly recommended; most friendly exhaust & tire shops will let you put a car on a lift for 5 minutes or so. If you can work this into your test drive that would be ideal and will convince the seller you're serious and that you may be an expert. The following items are easiest to check with the vehicle on a ramp or lift.

### Fuel system

The fuel tank is mounted below the rear passenger seat and straddles the transmission tunnel and driveshaft. Access to the in-tank fuel pump is under the seat cushion. Check the metal fuel feed and return lines for any damage, and ensure the protective plastic fuel filter cover is in place. All fuel pipes should be securely

The fuel pipes, brake pipes, hoses and parking brake cables are all routed in their correct factory locations, as shown in this useful overview shot. (Courtesy Alex Fearn)

fastened on the driver's side chassis rail, visible from underneath the LH side.

### Chassis rails & floors

☑4 ☑3 ☑2 ☑1

Fully inspect the length frame rails which extend from the front cross-member to the firewall, then drop down under the floor roughly in line with the transmission bell-housing. The floorpan and chassis rails extend rearwards to the lower control arms mountings, then kick up and over the axle, continuing across the trunk floor to the rear cross-member.

Check for any damage, deformation or the onset of corrosion to these key structural areas, paying special attention to the front sections between the front cross-member and bulkhead. Wrinkled or deformed metal here could indicate previous frontal impact damage.

### Brake pipes, hoses & cables

☑4 ☑3 ☑2 ☑1

Visually inspect all solid brake pipes for possible leaks, damage, corrosion and security. Check the flexible brake hoses looking for potential rubbing or interference. Lastly check the routing of the parking brake cables. Ideally all pipes, hoses and cables will be securely fastened and neatly routed in their factory positions.

### Exhaust system

☑4 ☑3 ☑2 ☑1

Visually inspect the pipes for any damage, and look for any corrosion or deterioration of the mufflers or catalytic converter casings. The exhaust should be securely mounted on the factory isolators and show no evidence of leaking (blowing).

A common upgrade is to replace the rear mufflers in search of a more muscular sound and louder exhaust note, which can be great fun, but this can wear off quickly on a long drive, and the added noise could annoy your neighbours.

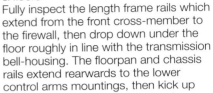

The exhaust system shown on this 2009 Shelby GT500KR is in great shape. Note the cylindrical axle-back mufflers. (Courtesy Alex Fearn)

## Evaluation procedure

Add up the total points:
Score: 224 = excellent; 168 = good; 112 = average; 56 = poor.

Cars scoring over 157 will be completely usable and will require only maintenance and care to preserve condition. Cars scoring between 56 and 114 will require some serious work (at much the same cost regardless of score). Cars scoring between 115 and 156 will require very careful assessment of the necessary repair/restoration costs in order to arrive at a realistic value.

# 10 Auctions
– sold! Another way to buy your dream

## Auction pros & cons

**Pros:** Prices will usually be lower than those of dealers or private sellers and you might grab a real bargain on the day. Auctioneers have usually established clear title with the seller. At the venue you can usually examine documentation relating to the vehicle.

**Cons:** You have to rely on a sketchy catalogue description of condition & history. The opportunity to inspect is limited and you cannot drive the car. Auction cars are often a little below par and may require some work. It's easy to overbid. There will usually be a buyer's premium to pay in addition to the auction hammer price.

## Which auction?

Auctions by established auctioneers are advertized in car magazines and on the auction houses' websites. A catalogue, or printed list of the lots might only be available a day or two ahead, though they are often listed and pictured on websites much earlier. Contact the auctioneers to ask if previous auction prices are available as this is useful information (details of sales are often available on websites).

## Catalogue, entry fee & payment details

When you purchase the catalogue of the vehicles in the auction, it often acts as a ticket allowing two people to attend the viewing days and the auction. Catalogue details tend to be comparatively brief, but will include information such as 'one owner from new, low mileage, full service history,' etc. It will also usually show a guide price to give you some idea of what to expect to pay, and tell you what is charged as a 'Buyer's premium.' Catalogues also contain details of acceptable forms of payment. At the fall of the hammer an immediate deposit is usually required, the balance payable within 24 hours. If the plan is to pay by cash, there may be a cash limit. Some auctions will accept payment by debit card. Sometimes credit or charge cards are acceptable, but will often incur an extra charge. A bank draft or bank transfer will have to be arranged in advance with your own bank, as well as with the auction house. No car will be released before all payments are cleared. If delays occur in payment transfers then storage costs can accrue.

## Buyer's premium

A buyer's premium will be added to the hammer price: don't forget this in your calculations. It is not usual for there to be a further state tax or local tax on the purchase price and/or on the buyer's premium.

## Viewing

In some instances it's possible to view on the day, or days before, as well as in the hours prior to the auction. There are auction officials available who are willing to help by opening engine and luggage compartments, and to allow you to inspect the interior. While the officials may start the engine for you, a test drive is out of the question. Crawling under and around the car as much as you want is permitted, but you can't suggest that the car you are interested in be jacked up, or attempt to do the job yourself. You can also ask to see any documentation available.

## Bidding

Before you take part in the auction, decide your maximum bid – and stick to it!

It may take a while for the auctioneer to reach the lot you are interested in, so use that time to observe how other bidders behave. When it's the turn of your car, attract the auctioneer's attention and make an early bid. The auctioneer will then look to you for a reaction every time another bid is made, usually the bids will be in fixed increments until the bidding slows, when smaller increments will often be accepted before the hammer falls. If you want to withdraw from the bidding, make sure the auctioneer understands your intentions – a vigorous shake of the head when he or she looks to you for the next bid should do the trick!

Assuming that you are the successful bidder, the auctioneer will note your card or paddle number, and from that moment on you will be responsible for the vehicle.

If the car is unsold, either because it failed to reach the reserve or because there was little interest, it may be possible to negotiate with the owner, via the auctioneers, after the sale is over.

## Successful bid

There are two more items to think about. How to get the car home, and insurance. If you can't drive the car, your own or a hired trailer is one way, another is to have the vehicle shipped using the facilities of a local company. The auction house will also have details of companies specializing in the transfer of cars.

Insurance for immediate cover can usually be purchased on site, but it may be more cost-effective to make arrangements with your own insurance company in advance, and then call to confirm the full details.

## eBay & other online auctions?

eBay and other online auctions could land you a car at a bargain price, though you'd be foolhardy to bid without examining the car first, something most vendors encourage. A useful feature of eBay is that the geographical location of the car is shown, so you can narrow your choices to those within a realistic radius of home. Be prepared to be outbid in the last few moments of the auction. Remember, your bid is binding and that it will be very, very difficult to get restitution in the case of a crooked vendor fleecing you – caveat emptor!

Be aware that some cars offered for sale in online auctions are 'ghost' cars. Don't part with any cash without being sure that the vehicle does actually exist and is as described (usually pre-bidding inspection is possible).

# 11 Paperwork
– correct documentation is essential!

## The paper trail
While S197 Mustangs are considered as modern classics, they can also be considered as collector or prestige cars (particularly outside the USA and Canada). Most cars should come with a portfolio of paperwork accumulated and passed on by successive owners. This documentation represents the service history of the car, and from it can be deduced the level of care the car has received, how much it's been used, which specialists have worked on it and the dates of major servicing or repair work. All of this information will be priceless to you as the new owner, so be wary of cars with little paperwork to support their claimed history.

## Registration documents
All countries/states have some form of registration for private vehicles whether it is like the American 'pink slip' system or the British 'log book' system.

It is essential to check that the registration document is genuine, that it relates to the car in question and that all the vehicle's details are correctly recorded, including chassis/VIN and engine numbers (if these are shown). If you are buying from the previous owner, his or her name and address will be recorded in the document: this will not be the case if you are buying from a dealer.

In the UK the current (Euro-aligned) registration document is named 'V5C,' and is printed in colored sections. The first section relates to the car specification, the second section has details of the new owner, and the third section is sent to the DVLA in the UK when the car is sold. A small additional section deals with selling the car within the motor trade.

In the UK the DVLA will provide details of earlier keepers of the vehicle upon payment of a small fee, and much can be learned in this way.

If the car has a foreign registration there may be expensive and time-consuming formalities to complete. Do you really want the hassle?

## Roadworthiness certificate
Many country/state administrations require that vehicles are regularly tested to prove that they are safe to use on the public highway, and do not produce excessive emissions. In the UK that test (the 'MoT') is carried out at approved testing stations, for a fee. In the USA the requirement varies by jurisdiction, but most states insist on an emissions test every two years as a minimum, while the police are charged with pulling over unsafe looking vehicles.

In the UK the test is required on an annual basis, once a vehicle becomes three years old. Of particular relevance for older cars is that the certificate issued includes the mileage reading recorded at the test date and, therefore, becomes an independent record of that car's history. Ask the seller if previous certificates are available. Without an MoT the vehicle should be trailered to its new home, unless you insist that a valid MoT is part of the deal. (Not such a bad idea this, as at least you will know the car was roadworthy on the day it was tested, and you don't need to wait for the old certificate to expire before having the test done.)

## Road license

The administration of every country/state charges some kind of taxation for the use of its road system. The actual form of the 'road license' and how it is displayed will vary country to country and state to state.

Whatever the form of the 'road license,' it must relate to the vehicle carrying it, and must be present and valid if the car is to be legally driven on the public highway. The value of the license will depend on the length of time it will continue to be valid.

In the UK if a car is untaxed because it has not been used for a period of time, the owner has to inform the licensing authorities, otherwise the vehicle's date-related registration number will be lost, and there will be a painful amount of paperwork to get it re-registered.

## Certificates of authenticity

For certain collectible models, like the GT/CS, Bullitt, Boss 302 and Shelby GT500 it is possible to get a 'certificate of authenticity' for a particular vehicle. Similarly, it is possible to obtain a breakdown of the production specification, which are sometimes called 'Build sheets' or 'Window Stickers,' and if the car comes with one of these it is a definite bonus. If you wish to obtain one for your vehicle, the 'Ford Show Parts' website (details in Chapter 16) or relevant local owners' club are good starting points.

## Valuation certificate

In some cases, the vendor will have a valuation certificate, or letter signed by a recognized expert stating how much he, or she, believes the particular car to be worth (such documents, together with photos, are usually needed to get 'agreed value' insurance). This may certainly be the case if the vehicle is one of the limited edition models, or has been highly modified or customized. Generally such documents should only act as confirmation of your own assessment of the car, rather than a guarantee of value, as the expert has probably not seen the car in the flesh. The easiest way to find out how to obtain a formal valuation is to contact the owners' club.

## Service history

Try to obtain as much service history and other paperwork pertaining to the car as you can. Naturally, dealer stamps, or specialist garage receipts score most points in the value stakes. However, anything helps in the great authenticity game; items like the original bill of sale, handbook, parts invoices and repair bills all add to the story and the character of the car. Even a brochure correct to the year of the car's manufacture is a useful document and something that you could well have to search hard to locate in future years. If the seller claims that the car has had major repair work or performance upgrades added, expect receipts and other evidence from a reputable shop.

If the seller claims to have carried out regular servicing, ask what work was completed and when, seek some evidence of it being carried out. Your assessment of the car's overall condition should tell you whether the seller's claims are genuine.

# 12 What's it worth?
– let your head rule your heart

If the car you've been looking at is in desperate need of repair or expensive remedial work, you may not have used the marking system provided in Chapter 9. If you have used the marking system, you should have a good idea if the car is in excellent, good, average or poor condition, or possibly sitting right between two categories.

Many specialist magazines run a pricing guide, which can be a handy reference when looking to compare current market values. Look at similar cars to the model you're thinking of buying, and also check values reported at auction houses. Some magazines have differing opinions of condition and value for certain models, so take this into account. If the car you're viewing is a local show winner with photographs and trophies to boot, it is possible that the advertized value will be higher than those listed in magazines. The same can also be said for a vehicle that has some kind of historical or significant motor-racing heritage. Assuming this is not the case, use your assessment to judge the price range, comparing to your online, magazine and auction reference material, and how this compares with the asking price. Don't forget to take into account the effect on the value and insurance premiums if there is any variation from standard specification.

When buying from a dealer, there will usually be a premium associated with the price.

## Desirable options/extras
The biggest factors affecting the value of an S197 Mustang are the model and engine options selected; it is definitely worth noting that desirable models – such as Shelby and Boss Mustangs – should have all of the correct details. While replication is the highest form of flattery, this can cause problems for would-be buyers if a 'clone' is passed off as a genuine car with an elevated asking price to match. Unfortunately, it's not uncommon for this to happen, so research the specific model you're looking for beforehand, particularly if it's one of the limited Bullitt, Boss or Shelby models.

Some performance-related options may also demand higher values, eg, a 2011 GT with the standard two-piston front brake calipers may be less valuable than a similar 2011 GT that has the desirable Brembo front brake option.

Basic items, such as stereo upgrades, electrically adjustable driver's seats, and seat heaters have less impact on the vehicle's value. The overall condition and mileage for most cars has far more influence on the value than these items.

Some aftermarket upgrades can increase kerb appeal, eg a nice set of aftermarket wheels and lowering springs fitted to a sleek coupe may make the car more desirable than the standard wheels and suspension. Other performance-related upgrades can also increase the value, such as performance brakes, uprated suspension parts, or even a Supercharger being fitted. You should evaluate the vehicle as a whole, and also consider the impact on insurance premiums.

## Striking a deal
Use your assessment of the vehicle's condition, any required remedial work and the specification to form the basis for negotiation. Be realistic and don't be immovable, as a small compromise from either party can facilitate a deal acceptable to you both.

Be sure, once a deal has been struck, that both you and the seller fill out the necessary details within the registration document or pink slip.

# 13 Do you really want to restore?

– it'll take longer and cost more than you think

Given the relative newness of the S197 Mustang, it's unlikely that even the earliest of models would be considered for restoration as you would a 1960s or 1970s Mustang. The anti-corrosion protection, modern paints and composite parts generally mean that rust is not a major concern. However, this is not to say that older variants with higher mileage don't present an opportunity to buy a car at a lower price and, with a little effort, return the car to showroom, or better, condition.

Given the heritage and performance focus of the Mustang, it's not uncommon for people to buy a Mustang as a 'project car,' to take to shows or the track. So whether you're planning some performance modifications, or just buying a standard car that needs some work, there are some things you may wish to consider.

## Difficulty

Your first consideration should be whether you can complete much of the work required on your own, or do you need to outsource to a knowledgeable shop? Some basics, like simple oil changes and fitting new brake pads, are easy, but other tasks, like fitting lowering springs or a brake upgrade kit may be a different story. Certain jobs may be best left to professionals, unless you have both the tools and experience to do this yourself.

This subtly modified GT/CS convertible is the owner's pride and joy. The simple exterior appearance belies the powerful supercharged engine hidden under the hood. (Courtesy Ray Welch)

## Time

If you're in full time employment and plan to wrench on the car at weekends, be realistic about how much time things take, especially if there are tasks you've never undertaken before. It's good to overestimate and allow as much time as possible, because things rarely go according to plan. Items break, bolts can shear, threads can strip, and you will always find something small that you need to finish the job, but don't have.

If the car is your daily driver, consider whether you really can afford to take it off the road in order to get that respray done, or to send off those aluminum wheels to be refurbished.

## Money

Only the very luckiest of people don't have to worry about their budget. With the superb aftermarket support for the S197, the sky is the limit with what you can create. But in reality, your pocket and what you're able to afford is the real limit. Spend your hard earned money wisely. Don't blow your budget on that huge supercharger kit, but not have anything left to upgrade the brakes, or buy some lovely wheels and buy cheap budget tires.

Clear turn signals, new door mirrors, Roush rear spoiler, lowered suspension, upgraded brakes, larger wheels and tires all combine to give this GT a clean unique look. (Courtesy Ray Welch)

## Planning

If you're just returning a car to nice clean condition, or going the whole hog to build a weekend-racer or show winner, you should plan your project. Consider that like most modern vehicles require specialized tools and diagnostic equipment, do you have those tools? How much space do you have to work in? Will you be affected by poor weather or the seasons? What if your project is delayed? Some basic planning can help keep your project on track and on budget, the result could be your dream Mustang at the end.

For performance-minded enthusiasts, a multitude of upgrades are available, such as the Vortech centrifugal supercharger kit installed on this spotless Mustang GT. (Courtesy Ray Welch)

If your budget doesn't stretch quite that far, you can customize in other ways, as shown by the fantastic air-brushed parts within this GT's engine bay. (Courtesy Ray Welch)

# 14 Paint problems
– bad complexion, including dimples, pimples and bubbles

Paint faults generally occur due to lack of protection/maintenance, or to poor preparation prior to a respray or touch-up. Some of the following conditions may be present in the car you're looking at:

## Orange peel
This appears as an uneven paint surface, similar to the appearance of the skin of an orange. The fault is caused by the failure of atomized paint droplets to flow into each other when they hit the surface. It is sometimes possible to rub out the effect with proprietary paint cutting/rubbing compound or very fine grades of abrasive paper. A respray may be necessary in severe cases. Consult a bodywork repairer/paint shop for advice on the particular car.

The uneven paint surface shown behind the cobra emblem on this 2010 Shelby GT500 is another example of 'orange peel.' (Courtesy Ray Welch)

Orange peel: with a lot of time and effort this can sometimes be resolved with cutting, rubbing and repolishing.

## Cracking
Severe cases are likely to have been caused by too heavy an application of paint (or filler beneath the paint). Also, insufficient stirring of the paint before application can lead to the components being improperly mixed, and cracking can result. Incompatibility with the paint already on the panel can have a similar effect. To rectify the problem it is necessary to rub down to a smooth, sound finish before respraying the problem area.

## Crazing
Sometimes the paint takes on a crazed rather than a cracked appearance when the problems mentioned under 'Cracking' are present. This problem can also be caused by a reaction between the underlying surface and the paint. Paint removal and respraying the problem area is usually the only solution.

While it's not an S197, this 1970 Mustang convertible shows a good example of paint cracking and resultant peeling.

## Blistering

Almost always caused by the corrosion of the metal beneath the paint. Usually, perforation will be found in the metal, and the damage will usually be worse than that suggested by the area of blistering. The metal will have to be repaired before repainting.

## Micro blistering

Usually the result of an economy respray where inadequate heating has allowed moisture to settle on the car before spraying. Consult a paint specialist, but, usually, damaged paint will have to be removed before partial or full respraying. This can also be caused by car covers that do not 'breathe.'

## Fading

Some colors, especially reds, are prone to fading if subjected to strong sunlight for long periods without the benefit of polish protection. Sometimes proprietary paint restorers and/or paint cutting/rubbing compounds will retrieve the situation. Often a respray is the only real solution.

## Peeling

Often a problem with metallic paintwork, when the sealing laquer becomes damaged and begins to peel off. Poorly applied paint may also peel. The remedy is to strip and start again!

The hood of this 2005 GT is showing signs of blistering caused by corrosion underneath the paint.

The underside of this hood really shows how the paint is blistering and beginning to peel away.

## Dimples

Dimples in the paintwork are caused by the residue of polish (particularly silicone types) not being removed properly before respraying. Paint removal and repainting is the only solution.

## Dents

Small dents are usually easily cured by the 'Dentmaster,' or equivalent process, that sucks or pushes out the dent (as long as the paint surface is still intact). Companies offering dent removal services usually come to your home: consult your telephone directory.

# 15 Problems due to lack of use

– just like their owners, Mustangs need exercise!

All vehicles, if not used regularly, can develop problems, and Mustangs aren't any different. Ford actually has a section entitled 'vehicle storage' within the owner's manual, which is aimed at keeping the vehicle in good operating condition if stored for a period of time.

If left connected, the battery's charge will drain over a period of time, as the security system and stereo system memory will always use a small amount of power, if left for an extended period, this can prevent starting. If the car is to be stored more than 30 days, disconnecting the battery is a good precautionary step to prevent this from happening. This is recommended in the owner's manual, which also points out that if the battery is disconnected, it will be necessary to reset memory features.

**This owner of this 2005 GT uses a battery conditioner over the winter months to ensure it remains in tip-top condition.**

Electrical contacts, if exposed to high humidity or moisture in the atmosphere, can suffer from corrosion, leading to poor contacts and potentially non-functional circuits. This is particularly true for battery terminals, where an insulating layer of corrosion can build up, resulting in a poor electrical connection.

Similarly, any raw aluminium or chromed parts, including polished wheels, brake calipers and engine components/accessories can suffer from corrosion if allowed to sit exposed to damp or moist air. This can ruin the finish of your lovely polished wheels and other components. This can be a particular problem if the vehicle is stored in a garage during the cold winter months.

Common glycol-ether-based brake fluid is hygroscopic, meaning that it can absorb or attract water from the surrounding environment or atmosphere. This has a detrimental effect on the boiling point of the fluid, and can also promote corrosion within the braking system components. This is why it is a good idea to replace/renew the brake fluid periodically or if repairs are required.

If left unchecked, or unused for a long period of time, brake caliper pistons can seize, or stick in their bores. Similarly, hand or parking brake cables and mechanisms can also seize, which is common on cars equipped with automatic transmissions, as many drivers rely on the parking pawl within the transmission. If storing the car for a long period, it's recommended to ensure the parking brake is left disengaged.

Fuel systems can also be a problem area. Modern in-tank fuel pumps can seize if left unused for long periods, resulting in a no-run condition. Fuel can also go stale – a problem which is aggravated by the increase of additives

These front brake parts have been removed to replace the corroded rotors and fit new pads. This type of surface rust can develop if stored outside and not used regularly.

like ethanol that is blended in modern fuels with the intention of improving the octane rating. It's best to fill up the fuel tank if storing the vehicle for a long time, and consider using a fuel stabilizer additive in line with Ford's recommendations.

If left for prolonged periods without use or rotation, the lubricating oil can drain away from internal metal components of the engine, leaving them exposed to potential moisture and corrosion. The same is true for transmissions and differentials; regular use is the only real preventative.

Rubber components such as hoses can shrink, perish and crack, making them unsafe under higher pressures, or, worse, they can develop leaks. This is especially important on flexible brake hoses and those within the fuel system. It's also recommended to regularly run the air-conditioning system, to ensure the seals don't shrink and to keep the clutch and compressor in working order.

Tires can develop flat spots if the vehicle is left standing in the same position for a long time, similarly the rubber can begin to perish and cracks can develop in the sidewall and tread areas. This is especially common if the car is left outside and exposed to the sun's ultraviolet (UV) rays.

# 16 The Community

– key people, organisations and companies in the Mustang world

## Clubs

Here are a few of the many Mustang clubs and groups around the world, but there are countless others. Seek out your local club and share the enjoyment and experiences of Mustang ownership with other great like-minded people.

Mustang Club of America (MCA)
http://www.mustang.org
Shelby American Automobile Club (SAAC)
http://www.saac.com
Mustang Owners Club of Great Britain (MOCGB)
http://www.mocgb.net
First Mustang Club of Germany (FMCoG)
http://www.ponysite.de/fmcog/
Classic Mustang Club of Sweden
http://www.mustangclubsweden.org
Norsk Mustang Club
http://www.norskmustangclub.no
Mustang Club of Denmark
http://www.mustangklubben.dk
Mustang Club de France
http://www.mustangclubdefrance.com

Belgian Mustang & Cougar Club (BMCC)
http://www.bmccweb.be
Mustang club of Switzerland
http://www.fordmustang.ch
Mustang club of Italy
http://mustangclubofitaly.it
Mustang owners club, Western Cape – South Africa
http://www.mustangwc.co.za
Mustang owners club of Australia
http://www.mustang.org.au
Mustang Club México
http://www.mustangclubmexico.com.mx  http://www.mustangclubmexico.com.mx
Canadian Mustang owners club
http://www.cmoc.ca  http://www.cmoc.ca

## Specialists

There are numerous specialists worldwide who deal with these iconic vehicles, many people have had very successful careers specializing in parts and apparel for Ford Mustang enthusiasts. The aftermarket industries continue to flourish and grow, fuelled by new blood and a whole other generation who have fallen in love with these pony cars and their cousins from the other US motor city manufacturers. Below is a short list of just a few of them.

American Muscle
California Pony Cars
CJ Pony Parts
Dallas Mustang
Ford Racing Parts
Late Model Restoration
Lethal Performance

Marti Auto Works
MMR – Modular Motorsports
Mustangs Unlimited
Roush Performance
Saleen
Shelby American
Steeda Autosports

## Motorsport

Since their introduction, Mustangs have been synonymous with performance and motorsport. You can get involved as well, with track days at local drag-racing strips and racing circuits. You don't have to spend a lot of money on upgrades or equipment to enjoy a Mustang at the track, just a few basic safety essentials. Whichever discipline you choose, drag racing, hill-climbing or circuit racing there's one thing for certain, Mustangs draw a crowd and you'll quickly meet other enthusiasts on and off the track.

## Websites

The Mustang Source
http://themustangsource.com
All Ford Mustangs
http://www.allfordmustangs.com
Mustangs Daily
http://mustangsdaily.com
Mustang Evolution
http://www.mustangevolution.com
S197 forum.com
http://www.s197forum.com
Mustang Forum.uk
http://www.mustangforum.uk
Mustang 360°
http://www.mustangandfords.com

StangNet
http://www.stangnet.com
BOSS Mustangs Online
http://bossmustangsonline.com
Boss 302 Forum & Club
http://www.boss302forum.com
Ford GT500.com
http://www.fordgt500.com
Team Shelby
http://www.teamshelby.com
SVT Performance.com
http://www.svtperformance.com
Ford Show Parts
http://www.fordshowparts.com

## Books & magazines

*Mustang Monthly Magazine*:
A great read every month with excellent features and technical and how-to articles written by some of the most respected Mustang enthusiasts in the business. Covers all generations of the Ford Mustang, all the time.

*Muscle Mustangs & Fast Fords*:
Monthly magazine which features all late model Fords, with great articles, tech information and numerous advertisements from specialists and part suppliers it's a good read and a useful source of information to boot.

*Red Book, Ford Mustang 1964½-2015* by Peter Sessler:
A great reference for production numbers, specifications, options, paint codes and other useful information.

*Weekend Projects for your Mustang 2005-Today* by Dan Sanchez and Drew Phillips:
A useful reference guide for S197 Mustang enthusiasts who're thinking about modifying and personalising their Mustang.

# 17 Vital statistics
– essential data at your fingertips

## Build numbers

2005 = 159,587
2006 = 165,762
2007 = 174,417
2008 = 111,125
2009 = 46,619

2010 = 81,508
2011 = 69,091
2012 = 88,392
2013 = 84,705
2014 = 134,082
**Total from 2005-2014 = 1,115,288**

## General specifications

|  | 2005 | 2006 | 2007 | 2008 | 2009 | 2010 | 2011 | 2012 | 2013 | 2014 |
|---|---|---|---|---|---|---|---|---|---|---|
| **Chassis** | Steel Monocoque/Unibody | | | | | | | | | |
| **Wheelbase** | 107.1in/2.720m | | | | | | | | | |
| **Overall length** | Coupe = 187.6in/4.765m<br>Convertible = 188.0in/4.775m | | | | | Coupe = 188.1in/4.778m | | | | |
| **Overall width [incl. mirrors]** | 73.8in/1.875m<br>[79.3in/2.014m] | | | | | 73.9in/1.877m<br>[80.1in/2.035m] | | | | |
| **Overall height** | Coupe = 55.4in/1.407m<br>Convertible = 55.7in/1.414m | | | | | Coupe = 55.8in/1.417m | | | | |

## Front suspension

Independent McPherson strut with 'reverse-L' lower control arms and tubular stabilizer (anti-roll) bar.

## Rear suspension

Three-link solid (live) axle with coil springs, tubular dampers (shock absorbers), panhard rod and solid stabilizer (anti-roll) bar.

## Steering

2005-2010 Rack and pinion with power assist (PAS). Ratio = 15.7:1
2011–2014 Selectable effort electric power assist steering (EPAS). Ratio = 15.9:1

## Rear axle type

7.5in, 28-spline axles with conventional (open) differential - V6 models from 2005-2010.
8.8in, 31-spline axles with limited slip differential – all V8 models and V6 models from 2011 onwards.
An optional Torsen differential upgrade was available on 2013/14 GT, 2013/14 Shelby GT500 and 2012/13 Boss 302 models.

## Brakes

Front
4-wheel disc brakes. Four-channel anti-lock braking system (ABS) with traction control on V8 powered models. For 2010 onwards, all models received the four-wheel 'AdvanceTrac' dynamic stability and traction control system.

V6 models:
2005-2010 = 11.5in (290mm) ventilated rotors/discs, with aluminum dual piston floating calipers.
2011-2014 = 12.4in (316mm) ventilated rotors/discs, with aluminum dual piston floating calipers.
GT – Standard equipment:
2005-2010 = 12.4in (316mm) ventilated rotors/discs, with aluminum dual piston floating calipers.
2011-2014 = 13.2in (335mm) ventilated rotors/discs, with aluminum dual piston floating calipers.
2012/13 Boss 302 and 2007-12 Shelby GT500 (optional on 2011-14 GT models):
14in (355mm) vented front rotors/discs and aluminum Brembo 4-piston fixed calipers
2013/14 Shelby GT500 only:
15in (380mm) vented front discs/rotors with aluminum Brembo 6-piston fixed calipers.

Rear
2005-14 Standard equipment on all models (excl. 2013/14 Shelby GT500):
11.8in (300mm) ventilated discs/rotors with aluminum single piston floating calipers and integral hand/parking brake mechanism.
2013/14 Shelby GT500 only:
13.8in (350mm) ventilated discs/rotors with aluminum single piston floating calipers and integral hand/parking brake mechanism.

**Wheels**
5 x 4.5in (114.3mm) PCD.
2005-2009 V6 & GT:
V6 = 16in x 7in aluminum.
V8 GT (standard) = 17in x 8in aluminum.
V8 GT (optional) = 18in aluminum.
2010-2014 V6 & GT:
V6 = 17in aluminum.
V6 w/performance package = 19in aluminum.
V8 GT (standard) = 18in aluminum.
V8 GT (optional) = 19in aluminum.
Shelby GT500:
2007-2009 GT500 = 18in x 9.5in bright machined aluminum.
2008/09 GT500KR = 18in x 9.5in, bright polished forged aluminum.
2010 GT500 convertible = 18in x 9.5in bright machined aluminum.
2010 GT500 coupe = 19in x 9.5in premium painted aluminum.
2011/12 = 19in x 9.5in, painted forged aluminum.
2011/12 w/SVT perf. package = 19in x 9.5in front, 20in x 9.5in rear, forged aluminum.
2013/14 = 19in x 9.5in front, 20in x 9.5in rear, forged aluminum.
Boss 302:
Standard = 19in x 9in front, 19in x 9.5in rear, black multi-spoke aluminum.
2012 Laguna Seca = 19in x 9in front, 19in x 10in rear, red/silver 10-spoke aluminum.
2013 Laguna Seca = 19in x 9in front, 19in x 10in rear, grey/silver 10-spoke aluminum.

# Engine

| | 2005 | | 2006 | |
|---|---|---|---|---|
| **Model** | V6 | GT | V6 | GT |
| **Engine code** | N | H | N | H |
| **Notes** | | | | |
| **Type** | 60-degree V6 | 90-degree V8 | 60-degree V6 | 90-degree V8 |
| **Family** | Cologne V6 | Modular 3V | Cologne V6 | Modular 3V |
| **Valvetrain configuration** | SOHC | SOHC with VCT | SOHC | SOHC with VCT |
| **Valves per cylinder** | 2-valve | 3-valve | 2-valve | 3-valve |
| **Block/heads** | Iron/aluminum | Aluminum/aluminum | Iron/aluminum | Aluminum/aluminum |
| **Displacement** | 4.0L (221ci) | 4.6L (281ci) | 4.0L (221ci) | 4.6L (281ci) |
| **Max. power** | 210bhp (157kW) @ 5300rpm | 300bhp (224kW) @ 5750rpm | 210bhp (157kW) @ 5300rpm | 300bhp (224kW) @ 5750rpm |
| **Max. torque** | 240lb/ft (325 N·m) @ 3500rpm | 320lb/ft (434 N·m) @ 4500rpm | 240lb/ft (325 N·m) @ 3500rpm | 320lb/ft (434 N·m) @ 4500rpm |
| **Transmission** | 5-speed manual - T5 5-speed auto (opt) - 5R55S | 5-speed manual - TR-3650 5-speed auto (opt) - 5R55S | 5-speed manual - T5 5-speed auto (opt) - 5R55S | 5-speed manual - TR-3650 5-speed auto (opt) - 5R55S |
| **Axle type** | 7.5in, 28-spline axles. Open differential | 8.8in, 31-spline axles. Traction-Lok, LSD | 7.5in, 28-spline axles. Open differential | 8.8in, 31-spline axles. Traction-Lok, LSD |
| **[Axle code] axle ratio** | [BG] 3.31 | [CD] 3.55 [CG] 3.31 (w/AT) | [BG] 3.31 | [CD] 3.55 [CG] 3.31 (w/AT) |

| | 2007 | | |
|---|---|---|---|
| **Model** | V6 | GT | Shelby GT500 |
| **Engine code** | N | H | S |
| **Notes** | | | |
| **Type** | 60-degree V6 | 90-degree V8 | 90-degree supercharged V8 |
| **Family** | Cologne V6 | Modular 3V | Modular 4V |
| **Valvetrain configuration** | SOHC | SOHC with VCT | DOHC |
| **Valves per cylinder** | 2-valve | 3-valve | 4-valve |
| **Block/heads** | Iron/aluminum | Aluminum/aluminum | Iron/aluminum |
| **Displacement** | 4.0L (221ci) | 4.6L (281ci) | 5.4L (330ci) |
| **Max. power** | 210bhp (157kW) @ 5300rpm | 300bhp (224kW) @ 5750rpm | 500bhp (373kW) @ 6000rpm |
| **Max. torque** | 240lb/ft (325Nm) @ 3500rpm | 320lb/ft (434Nm) @ 4500rpm | 480lb/ft (651Nm) @ 4500rpm |
| **Transmission** | 5-speed manual - T5 5-speed auto (opt) - 5R55S | 5-speed manual - TR-3650 5-speed auto (opt) - 5R55S | 6-speed manual - TR-6060 |
| **Axle type** | 7.5in, 28-spline axles. Open differential | 8.8in, 31-spline axles. Traction-Lok, LSD | 8.8in, 31-spline axles. Traction-Lok, LSD |
| **[Axle code] axle ratio** | [BG] 3.31 | [CG] 3.31 [CD] 3.55 (opt. MT only) | [CG] 3.31 |

| 2008 | | | | | |
|---|---|---|---|---|---|
| **Model** | **V6** | **GT and GT/CS** | **Bullitt** | **Shelby GT500** | **Shelby GT500KR** |
| **Engine code** | N | H | H | S | S |
| **Notes** | | | Limited edition | | Limited edition |
| **Type** | 60-degree V6 | 90-degree V8 | 90-degree V8 | 90-degree supercharged V8 | 90-degree supercharged V8 |
| **Family** | Cologne V6 | Modular 3V | Modular 3V | Modular 4V | Modular 4V |
| **Valvetrain configuration** | SOHC | SOHC with VCT | SOHC with VCT | DOHC | DOHC |
| **Valves per cylinder** | 2-valve | 3-valve | 3-valve | 4-valve | 4-valve |
| **Block/heads** | Iron/aluminum | Aluminum/aluminum | Aluminum/aluminum | Iron/aluminum | Iron/aluminum |
| **Displacement** | 4.0L (221ci) | 4.6L (281ci) | 4.6L (281ci) | 5.4L (330ci) | 5.4L (330ci) |
| **Max. power** | 210bhp (157kW) @ 5300rpm | 300bhp (224kW) @ 5750rpm | 315bhp (235kW) @ 6000rpm | 500bhp (373kW) @ 6000rpm | 540bhp (403kW) @ 6000rpm |
| **Max. torque** | 240lb/ft (325Nm) @ 3500rpm | 320lb/ft (434Nm) @ 4500rpm | 325lb/ft (441Nm) @ 4250rpm | 480lb/ft (651Nm) @ 4500rpm | 510lb/ft (691Nm) @ 4500rpm |
| **Transmission** | 5-speed manual - T5 5-speed auto (opt) - 5R55S | 5-speed manual - TR-3650 | 5-speed auto (opt) - 5R55S 5-speed manual - TR-3650 | 6-speed manual - TR-6060 | 6-speed manual - TR-6060 |
| **Axle type** | 7.5in, 28-spline axles. Open differential | 8.8in, 31-spline axles. Traction-Lok, LSD | 8.8in, 31-spline axles. Traction-Lok, LSD | 8.8in, 31-spline axles. Traction-Lok, LSD | 8.8in, 31-spline axles. Traction-Lok, LSD |
| **[Axle code] axle ratio** | [BG] 3.31 | [CG] 3.31 [CD] 3.55 (opt. MT only) | [CB] 3.73 | [CG] 3.31 | [CB] 3.73 |

| 2009 | | | | | |
|---|---|---|---|---|---|
| **Model** | **V6** | **GT and GT/CS** | **Bullitt** | **Shelby GT500** | **Shelby GT500KR** |
| **Engine code** | N | H | H | S | S |
| **Notes** | | | Limited edition | | Limited edition |
| **Type** | 60-degree V6 | 90-degree V8 | 90-degree V8 | 90-degree supercharged V8 | 90-degree supercharged V8 |
| **Family** | Cologne V6 | Modular 3V | Modular 3V | Modular 4V | Modular 4V |
| **Valvetrain configuration** | SOHC | SOHC with VCT | SOHC with VCT | DOHC | DOHC |
| **Valves per cylinder** | 2-valve | 3-valve | 3-valve | 4-valve | 4-valve |
| **Block/heads** | Iron/aluminum | Aluminum/aluminum | Aluminum/aluminum | Iron/aluminum | Iron/aluminum |
| **Displacement** | 4.0L (221ci) | 4.6L (281ci) | 4.6L (281ci) | 5.4L (330ci) | 5.4L (330ci) |
| **Max. power** | 210bhp (157kW) @ 5300rpm | 300bhp (224kW) @ 5750rpm | 315bhp (235kW) @ 6000rpm | 500bhp (373kW) @ 6000rpm | 540bhp (403kW) @ 6000rpm |
| **Max. torque** | 240lb/ft (325Nm) @ 3500rpm | 320lb/ft (434Nm) @ 4500rpm | 325lb/ft (441Nm) @ 4250rpm | 480lb/ft (651Nm) @ 4500rpm | 510lb/ft (691Nm) @ 4500rpm |

| 2009 (continued) | | | | | |
|---|---|---|---|---|---|
| Model | V6 | GT and GT/CS | Bullitt | Shelby GT500 | Shelby GT500KR |
| Transmission | 5-speed manual - T5 5-speed auto (opt) - 5R55S | 5-speed manual - TR-3650 5-speed auto (opt) - 5R55S | 5-speed manual - TR-3650 | 6-speed manual - TR-6060 | 6-speed manual - TR-6060 |
| Axle type | 7.5in, 28-spline axles. Open differential | 8.8in, 31-spline axles. Traction-Lok, LSD | 8.8in, 31-spline axles. Traction-Lok, LSD | 8.8in, 31-spline axles. Traction-Lok, LSD | 8.8in, 31-spline axles. Traction-Lok, LSD |
| [Axle code] axle ratio | [BG] 3.31 | [CG] 3.31 [CD] 3.55 (opt. MT only) | [CB] 3.73 | [CG] 3.31 | [CB] 3.73 |

| 2010 | | | |
|---|---|---|---|
| Model | V6 | GT | Shelby GT500 |
| Engine code | N | H | S |
| Notes | | | |
| Type | 60-degree V6 | 90-degree V8 | 90-degree supercharged V8 |
| Family | Cologne V6 | Modular 3V | Modular 4V |
| Valvetrain configuration | SOHC | SOHC with VCT | DOHC |
| Valves per cylinder | 2-valve | 3-valve | 4-valve |
| Block/heads | Iron/aluminum | Aluminum/aluminum | Iron/aluminum |
| Displacement | 4.0L (245ci) | 4.6L (281ci) | 5.4L (330ci) |
| Max. power | 210bhp (157kW) @ 5300rpm | 315bhp (235kW) @ 6000rpm | 540bhp (403kW) @ 6200rpm |
| Max. torque | 240lb/ft (325Nm) @ 3500rpm | 325lb/ft (441Nm) @ 4250rpm | 510lb/ft (691Nm) @ 4500rpm |
| Transmission | 5-speed manual - T5 5-speed auto (optional) - 5R55S | 5-speed manual - TR-3650 5-speed auto (optional) - 5R55S | 6-speed manual - TR-6060 |
| Axle type | 7.5in, 28-spline axles. Open differential | 8.8in, 31-spline axles. Traction-Lok, LSD | 8.8in, 31-spline axles. Traction-Lok, LSD |
| [Axle code] axle ratio | [BG] 3.31 | [CG] 3.31 [CD] 3.55 (opt. MT only) [CB] 3.73 (opt. MT only) | [CD] 3.55 |

| 2011 | | | |
|---|---|---|---|
| Model | V6 | GT and GT/CS | Shelby GT500 |
| Engine code | M | F | S |
| Notes | | | |
| Type | 90-degree V6 | 90-degree V8 | 90-degree supercharged V8 |
| Family | Duratec V6 | Modular 4V 'Coyote' | Modular 4V |

| 2011 (continued) | | | |
|---|---|---|---|
| Model | V6 | GT and GT/CS | Shelby GT500 |
| Valvetrain configuration | DOHC with Ti-VCT | DOHC with Ti-VCT | DOHC |
| Valves per cylinder | 4-valve | 4-valve | 4-valve |
| Block/heads | Aluminum/aluminum | Aluminum/aluminum | Aluminum/aluminum |
| Displacement | 3.7L | 5.0L (302ci) | 5.4L (330ci) |
| Max. power | 305bhp (227kW) @ 6500rpm | 412bhp (307kW) @ 6500rpm | 550bhp (410kW) @ 6200rpm |
| Max. torque | 280lb/ft (280Nm) @ 4250rpm | 390lb/ft (529Nm) @ 4250rpm | 510lb/ft (691Nm) @ 4250rpm |
| Transmission | 6-speed manual - MT82 6-speed auto (opt.) - 6R80 | 6-speed manual - MT82 6-speed auto (opt.) - 6R80 | 6-speed manual - TR-6060 |
| Axle type | 8.8in, 31-spline axles. Traction-Lok, LSD | 8.8in, 31-spline axles. Traction-Lok, LSD | 8.8in, 31-spline axles. Traction-Lok, LSD |
| [Axle code] axle ratio | [CC] 2.73 [GG] 3.31 (opt. coupe only) | [GG] 3.31 [YY] 3.15 (w/AT) [DD] 3.55 (opt. MT only) [BB] 3.73 (opt. MT only | [BB] 3.55 [BB] 3.73 (opt) |

| 2012 | | | | |
|---|---|---|---|---|
| Model | V6 | GT and GT/CS | Boss 302 | Shelby GT500 |
| Engine code | M | F | U | S |
| Notes | | | Engine codename: 'Road Runner' | |
| Type | 90-degree V6 | 90-degree V8 | 90-degree V8 | 90-degree supercharged V8 |
| Family | Duratec V6 | Modular 4V 'Coyote' | Modular 4V 'Coyote' | Modular 4V |
| Valvetrain configuration | DOHC with Ti-VCT | DOHC with Ti-VCT | DOHC with Ti-VCT | DOHC |
| Valves per cylinder | 4-valve | 4-valve | 4-valve | 4-valve |
| Block/heads | Aluminum/aluminum | Aluminum/aluminum | Aluminum/aluminum | Aluminum/aluminum |
| Displacement | 3.7L (227ci) | 5.0L (302ci) | 5.0L (302ci) | 5.4L (330ci) |
| Max. power | 305bhp (227kW) @ 6500rpm | 412bhp (307kW) @ 6500rpm | 444bhp (331kW) @ 7400rpm | 550bhp (410kW) @ 6200rpm |
| Max. torque | 280lb/ft (280Nm) @ 4250rpm | 390lb/ft (529Nm) @ 4250rpm | 380lb/ft (520Nm) @ 4500rpm | 510lb/ft (691Nm) @ 4250rpm |
| Transmission | 6-speed manual - MT82 6-speed auto (opt.) - 6R80 | 6-speed manual - MT82 6-speed auto (opt.) - 6R80 | 6-speed manual - MT82 | 6-speed manual - TR-6060 |
| Axle type | 8.8in, 31-spline axles. Traction-Lok, LSD | 8.8in, 31-spline axles. Traction-Lok, LSD | 8.8in, 31-spline axles. Traction-Lok, LSD | 8.8in, 31-spline axles. Traction-Lok, LSD |
| [Axle code] axle ratio | [CC] 2.73 [GG] 3.31 (opt. coupe only) | [GG] 3.31 [YY] 3.15 (w/AT) [DD] 3.55 (opt. MT coupe only) [BB] 3.73 (opt. MT coupe only) | [BB] 3.73 [BB] 3.73 w/Torsen (opt.) | [DD] 3.55 [BB] 3.73 (opt.) |

| 2013 | | | | |
|---|---|---|---|---|
| **Model** | **V6** | **GT and GT/CS** | **Boss 302** | **Shelby GT500** |
| **Engine code** | M | F | U | Z |
| **Notes** | | | Engine codename: 'Road Runner' | Project Codename: 'Trinity' |
| **Type** | 90-degree V6 | 90-degree V8 | 90-degree V8 | 90-degree V8 |
| **Family** | Duratec V6 | Modular 4V 'Coyote' | Modular 4V 'Coyote' | Modular 4V |
| **Valvetrain configuration** | DOHC with Ti-VCT | DOHC with Ti-VCT | DOHC with Ti-VCT | DOHC |
| **Valves per cylinder** | 4-valve | 4-valve | 4-valve | 4-valve |
| **Block/heads** | Aluminum/aluminum | Aluminum/aluminum | Aluminum/aluminum | Aluminum/aluminum |
| **Displacement** | 3.7L (227ci) | 5.0L (302ci) | 5.0L (302ci) | 5.8L (355ci) |
| **Max. power** | 305bhp (227kW) @ 6500rpm | 420bhp (313kW) @ 6500rpm | 444bhp (331kW) @ 7400rpm | 662bhp (494kW) @ 6500rpm |
| **Max. torque** | 280lb/ft (280Nm) @ 4250rpm | 390lb/ft (529Nm) @ 4250rpm | 380lb/ft (520Nm) @ 4500rpm | 631lb/ft (856Nm) @ 4000rpm |
| **Transmission** | 6-speed manual - MT82 6-speed auto (optional) - 6R80 | 6-speed manual - MT82 6-speed auto (optional) - 6R80 | 6-speed manual - MT82 | 6-speed manual - TR-6060 |
| **Axle type** | 8.8in, 31-spline axles. Traction-Lok, LSD | 8.8in, 31-spline axles. Traction-Lok, LSD | 8.8in, 31-spline axles. Traction-Lok, LSD | 8.8in, 31-spline axles. Traction-Lok, LSD |
| **[Axle code] axle ratio** | [CC] 2.73 [GG] 3.31 (opt. coupe only) | [GG] 3.31 [DD] 3.55 (opt. MT coupe only) [BB] 3.73 (opt. MT coupe only) [BB] 3.73 w/Torsen (opt. MT coupe only) | [BB] 3.73 [BB] 3.73 w/Torsen (opt.) | [GG] 3.31 [GG] 3.31 w/Torsen (opt.) |

| 2014 | | | |
|---|---|---|---|
| **Model** | **V6** | **GT and GT/CS** | **Shelby GT500** |
| **Engine code** | M | F | Z |
| **Notes** | | | Project Codename: 'Trinity' |
| **Type** | 90-degree V6 | 90-degree V8 | 90-degree V8 |
| **Family** | Duratec V6 | Modular 4V 'Coyote' | Modular 4V |
| **Valvetrain configuration** | DOHC with Ti-VCT | DOHC with Ti-VCT | DOHC |
| **Valves per cylinder** | 4-valve | 4-valve | 4-valve |
| **Block/heads** | Aluminum/aluminum | Aluminum/aluminum | Aluminum/aluminum |
| **Displacement** | 3.7L (227ci) | 5.0L (302ci) | 5.8L (355ci) |
| **Max. power** | 305bhp (227kW) @ 6500rpm | 420bhp (313kW) @ 6500rpm | 662bhp (494kW) @ 6500rpm |
| **Max. torque** | 280lb/ft (280Nm) @ 4250rpm | 390lb/ft (529Nm) @ 4250rpm | 631lb/ft (856Nm) @ 4000rpm |
| **Transmission** | 6-speed manual - MT82 6-speed auto (optional) - 6R80 | 6-speed manual - MT82 6-speed auto (optional) - 6R80 | 6-speed manual - TR-6060 |
| **Axle type** | 8.8in, 31-spline axles. Traction-Lok, LSD | 8.8in, 31-spline axles. Traction-Lok, LSD | 8.8in, 31-spline axles. Traction-Lok, LSD |
| **[Axle code] axle ratio** | [CC] 2.73 [GG] 3.31 (optional, coupe only) | [GG] 3.31 [DD] 3.55 (opt. MT coupe only) [BB] 3.73 (opt. MT coupe only) [BB] 3.73 w/Torsen (opt. MT coupe only) | [GG] 3.31 [GG] 3.31 w/Torsen (opt.) |

# The Essential Buyer's Guide™ series ...

978-1-845840-22-8

978-1-845840-26-6

978-1-845840-29-7

978-1-845840-77-8

978-1-845840-99-0

978-1-904788-70-6

978-1-845841-01-0

978-1-845841-19-5

978-1-845841-13-3

978-1-845841-35-5

978-1-845841-36-2

978-1-845841-38-6

978-1-845841-46-1

978-1-845841-47-8

978-1-845841-63-8

978-1-845841-65-2

978-1-845841-88-1

978-1-845841-92-8

978-1-845842-00-0

978-1-845842-04-8

978-1-845842-05-5

978-1-845842-70-3

978-1-845842-81-9

978-1-845842-83-3

978-1-845842-84-0

978-1-845842-87-1

978-1-84584-134-8

978-1-845843-03-8

978-1-845843-09-0

978-1-845843-16-8

978-1-845843-29-8

978-1-845843-30-4

978-1-845843-34-2

978-1-845843-38-0

978-1-845843-39-7

978-1-845841-61-4

978-1-845842-31-4

978-1-845843-07-6

978-1-845843-40-3

978-1-845843-48-9

978-1-845843-63-2

978-1-845844-09-7

# The Essential Buyer's Guide

**100,000+ COPIES SOLD THIS SERIES**

## FORD
# MUSTANG

First Generation 1964 to 1973

**VELOCE**

Your marque expert: Matt Cook

Having this book in your pocket is just like having a real marque expert by your side. Benefit from the author's years of Mustang ownership, learn how to spot a bad car quickly, and how to assess a promising car like a professional. Get the right car at the right price!

ISBN: 978-1-845844-47-9
Paperback • 19.5x13.9cm • £12.99* UK/$19.95* USA • 64 pages • 106 colour pictures

For more info on Veloce titles, visit our website at www.veloce.co.uk
• email: info@veloce.co.uk • Tel: +44(0)1305 260068
* prices subject to change, p&p extra

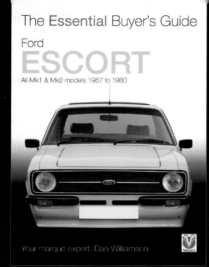

# Index